W9-BNO-347

"Jennifer Rothschild is one of our favorite *LIFE Today* guests. To be in her presence is to feel God's touch. Through personal stories and time-tested Scriptures, Jennifer inspires readers to get back to the basics and seek a fresh touch from God. Once we have been touched by the Master, we will never be the same again—and we'll want others to experience His life-changing touch."

JAMES ROBISON, FOUNDER AND PRESIDENT OF LIFE OUTREACH INTERNATIONAL

"Jennifer is a wise and gifted guide, and she takes us on a journey, in turns sidesplitting and heartrending, playful and urgent, straight to the heart of God. Prepare to discover—or rediscover—the One who longs to take hold of you and not let go until, wounded and mended, you are fully formed. Thank you, Jennifer, for helping us all to see our God as you do—with clearness, deepness, and such great love."

MARK BUCHANAN, AUTHOR OF *THINGS UNSEEN* AND *THE HOLY WILD*

"I appreciate the way Jennifer uses her 'weakness' to help the rest of us gain strength from overlooked biblical metaphors—in this case, the touch of God."

MARK GALLI, COAUTHOR OF *THE COMPLETE IDIOT'S GUIDE TO PRAYER*

"Perceptive and wise, Jennifer Rothschild writes from the heart with warmth and sensitivity. Reading *Touched by His Unseen Hand,* I felt like I was sitting across the table from her. Jennifer loves Jesus and will help you love Him too."

RANDY ALCORN, AUTHOR OF *THE PURITY PRINCIPLE*

JENNIFER
ROTHSCHILD

Multnomah® Publishers *Sisters, Oregon*

TOUCHED BY HIS UNSEEN HAND
published by Multnomah Publishers, Inc.

International Standard Book Number: 1-59052-210-9

Cover image by Edward Rosenberger/Workbookstock.com

Italicized words in Scripture passages indicate the author's emphasis.

Printed in the United States of America

For information:
MULTNOMAH PUBLISHERS, INC. • P. O. Box 1720 • SISTERS, OREGON 97759

04 05 06 07 08 09 10—10 9 8 7 6 5 4 3 2 1 0

I lovingly dedicate this book to
Dr. Philip Rothschild,
who has willingly been the hands of God
in my life for seventeen years.
Thank you for your gentleness and strength.

Contents

ONE

Fingerprints of God

Have you stood before a magnificent ocean, feeling its majestic power and misty thunder as it slaps the shoreline and drags the sand into its lair?

I have. And when I do, I feel very small.

The largeness of the ocean envelops my sense of frame. I feel as vulnerable as a twig, as ungrounded as a feather, as diminutive as a dust particle, floating and landing without notice, without effect.

This feeling of excessive smallness, of course, may

have something to do with my own state of vertical challenge. Oh yes, I'm often caught exaggerating that my stature is five feet three inches, when actually I'm just five feet two and two-thirds. (You'd be surprised how much self-esteem that one little third of an inch can add.) It wouldn't be such an exaggeration, anyway. When you include the hair poof atop my head and the three inches of chunky rubber beneath my heels, I'm really a towering five foot eight!

I've always wanted to be taller.

I've tried every way I know to elongate my spine as I walk or stand, executing my best model-like posture in an attempt to make up for my missing inches. I'm even short-waisted! There can't be more than two inches between my lowest rib and the top of my hip. I haven't tucked in a shirt for years. When I do, I just look like someone tried to compress me—my hips get wider, my legs squattier. It's awful!

In addition to my Zacchaeus complex, I've acquired other related maladies.

I'm often short-tempered.

I have a short memory. (Except when it comes to my husband's mistakes—those I can remember forever!)

I'm frequently shortsighted.

I'm also usually short on cash. And patience.

In the larger sense, however, we're all small. It doesn't

matter if you're a tall, willowy woman or some towering specimen of manhood. No matter what our vertical inches, we must all eventually recognize that we're pretty small potatoes.

The prophet had the right idea when he said of the Lord, "He sits enthroned above the circle of the earth, and its people are like grasshoppers" (Isaiah 40:22).

David understood as well. He was merely a boy, lowest on the family totem pole compared to his older brothers, when the prophet Samuel proclaimed he would one day rule Israel as king. He must have felt ridiculously undersized when King Saul sought to dress him in the royal armor to fight Goliath. He was swallowed by it, eventually shedding it for his simple garb. Years and years later, as a middle-aged king himself, the gentle psalmist must have felt the frailty of his stature as the man after God's heart broke God's heart in choosing Bathsheba rather than battle.

I wonder what it must have been like for him, even as a shepherd boy resting in the cleft of a rock, plucking his harp strings in the cool of the evening. Perhaps he looked across the silhouette of the surrounding Judean hills at dusk and thought of his smallness. Perhaps he gazed into the soft light of a star-blanketed sky and once again felt his size. Maybe it was then that he wrote, "When I consider your heavens, the work of your fingers, the moon and the stars, which you have set in place, what is man that you are mindful of him, the son of man that you care for him?" (Psalm 8:3–4).

Like David, we all should be more reflective. We should consider the grandeur that surrounds us and contemplate our own size within its scheme. Depressing, you say? Overwhelming? Not at all. In fact, the more we consider God's greatness and our smallness, the more we will marvel at the great value He has placed on our lives. Small, frail, earthbound, and fallen though we are, those who belong to Jesus Christ are greatly valued through all of time, and time beyond time. Not even a sparrow falls that our heavenly Father doesn't see. You and I are far more valuable than that tiny sparrow. God's signature of creation was written on the very heart and frame of man. We really are His workmanship.

It all began, of course, with God's spoken word. All the grandeur, all the majesty, all the wonder of a creation beyond our comprehension began with His voice. It began with the words in Genesis 1:3, where God said, "Let there be light." From there, He spoke His vast creation into existence. Planets and stars. Mountains and oceans. Forests and animals. Birds and sea creatures. Towering trees and tiny flowers. All creation was initiated by God's word.

All except man.

It was with His hand, His *touch,* that He crafted the crowning jewel of all His handiwork. "The LORD God formed the man from the dust of the ground and breathed into his nostrils the breath of life, and the man became a living being" (Genesis 2:7).

Later, He gently fashioned a woman from the rib of Adam with those same hands. He could have spoken you and me into existence, too. But He chose to use His hands. It is His touch that separates us from all created things. It is His touch that defines and honors us above all other created beings.

Does God, a Spirit, truly have hands as we have hands? I'll leave that one for the theologians to solve. I only know that Scripture differentiates the way He formed man and woman from every other created thing. It wasn't business as usual. I don't know exactly how He did it, but I do know there was a special touch.

And in that touch was honor.

I feel like David when I think of a glorious God breathing life into these earthen vessels. I'll bet you feel the same way. It's overwhelming to consider that it was His hand that formed and crafted us. The thought is disarming—that God would touch us and compassionately craft us according to His image. But sometimes, fixated as we become on our own frailty and flaws, we fail to recognize His touch or craftsmanship in our lives.

BROKEN BUT STILL VALUED

During my college years, a friend of mine gave me a very special gift. It was a beautiful Lladró porcelain figurine of a woman, with slender lines, adorned with a graceful hat and a vase of flowers. This delicate Lladró moved from city to city, from home to home, with my husband and me for the first seven years of our marriage. It was one of my most treasured possessions.

One fateful afternoon, though, our four-year-old son was playing a game of hide-and-seek near the table where the Lladró gracefully stood. A bump of the table sent her to the floor, chipping the tips of the petals on her flowers. We glued her dainty pieces back together as best we could, but her bouquet was never the same.

Many years have passed. Another city, another home. My beautiful Lladró has followed, and she still finds her home in our living room. I often wonder why I value her so—why she has a place of honor on my mantel.

She's flawed.

She's no longer smooth.

She's no longer perfect.

She's surely lost all monetary value.

I've come to realize that I value her because she reminds me of a person I know. I too am broken. I am imperfect. I've lost some of my slender lines. My bouquet has been chipped. In fact, we're *all* broken. We're all flawed. But we are still of value because Someone values us. Someone loves us and positions us in a place of honor. God continually honors us by the way He treats us. In fact, from the beginning of recorded time, we see the heart of God fixed upon us, His creation. In every book of the Bible, we see the value God places on us. We are reminded that He loves us and honors us with the wonder of His touch.

In Genesis, He fashions us with His hands. In Exodus, He gives us freedom and deliverance. In Leviticus, He gives us access to Himself. In Numbers, He builds cities of refuge to protect us. In Deuteronomy, He guides us with His protective hand. In Joshua, He honors us with the certainty of His divine purpose. In Judges, He shows mercy in spite of our repeated failures. In Ruth, He values us by bringing us into His family.

In 1 and 2 Samuel, He makes the insignificant significant. In 1 and 2 Kings, He honors us by His faithfulness toward us. In the books of the Chronicles, He makes our prayer powerful, granting us success. In Ezra and Nehemiah, He allows us to return to Him, gives us tools to rebuild all that is broken, and restores us to Himself.

In Esther, He gives us great purpose...and makes us royalty. In Job, He restores us after we've suffered and shows Himself strong on our behalf. In Psalms, He calls us closer to Himself and encourages us to sing in His presence. In Proverbs, He reveals His wisdom to us. In Ecclesiastes, He gives meaning to our meaninglessness. In Song of Solomon, He draws us to run after Him, the Lover of our souls.

In Isaiah, He reveals the Savior to us. In Jeremiah and Lamentations, He sees our tears and gives us hope of greater freedom. In Ezekiel and Daniel, the sovereign Lord joins us in the midst of the fire. In Hosea, God pursues us to buy us back. In Joel, He blesses us when we repent. In Amos, He bears our burdens. In Obadiah, He keeps His covenant to us. In Jonah, He honors us by using imperfect man to fulfill His own perfect plan. In Micah, He invites us to walk humbly with Him. In Nahum, He comforts us. In Habakkuk, He places our lowliness in high places. In Zephaniah, He sings over us with great joy. In Haggai, God Himself makes His dwelling among us. In Zechariah, God reveals His plans for the future and assures us of His coming. In Malachi, God shows us we can't out-give Him as He pours out His blessing.

In the four Gospels, God puts on human flesh just to seek and save us. In Acts, He pours out His Spirit on us, and in Romans, He works all things for our good! In the letters to the Corinthians, He pulls us from error, teaches us the way of love, and points us toward unseen realities. In Galatians, He sets us free! In Ephesians, He lavishes us with the riches of grace. In Philippians, He gives us victory and joy. In Colossians, we are rooted and strengthened in Him—and overflow with thankfulness. In the letters to the churches in Thessalonica, He honors us by giving us a future hope. In the letters to Timothy, He offers us counsel and encouragement. In Titus, He equips us for good works. In Philemon, He turns our slavery into brotherhood. In Hebrews, He invites us to come boldly before His throne. In James, He teaches us practical religion. In 1 and 2 Peter, He gives us victory over suffering. In the three epistles of John, He assures us of eternity and invites us to walk in His light, life, and love. In Jude, our God tenderly keeps us from falling and values us so highly that He Himself presents us faultless before His own throne. And then in Revelation, He bestows the ultimate honor upon us as He receives us as His beloved and treasured bride.

You are the reason He established and kept His covenant. You are the reason He grew a tree that became a cross. You are so valuable to Him that He is "not willing that any should perish but that all should come to repentance" (2 Peter 3:9, NKJV).

Have you recognized His touch? Do you believe that the value and honor He gives you make you complete? Never forget that you are so valuable you were worth dying for. Receive His touch and you will receive the honor and sense of value that you long for. After all, His eyes have always been on you. Your very life is covered with His fingerprints. Psalm 139 reminds us that our frame was not hidden from God when He knit us together in our mother's womb.

No matter how many miles we've walked in life's journey, His eyes have seen every step. Even when we don't feel valuable, we still *are* valuable. Even when we don't *feel* noticed, God's eyes never leave us. Even when we don't *feel* His touch, our lives reflect His hand. Even when darkness surrounds us, we can be sure that there is a God who sees us.

THE GOD WHO SEES

There was a woman who lived centuries ago who understood what it meant to be "seen" by God. She was a simple Egyptian slave girl named Hagar. When I asked my husband, a business professor, if he was familiar with the story of Hagar, he confidently announced, "Of course I am!" Then he proceeded to explain to me how decades ago a clever entrepreneur created and marketed a pair of leisure pants that would be both comfortable and professional for the American male. He went on to discuss their successful sales figures at J. C. Penney and their frequent appearance on *The Price Is Right.*

Well, that wasn't exactly the Hagar I was thinking of. But at least he didn't mention the portly cartoon Viking featured in the comic strips! These days, this lady from the pages of Scripture seems destined to play second fiddle to a cartoon character and a pair of pants. But let me tell you her story and about the honoring touch of God on the life of this female slave.

We find Hagar in Genesis 16. She belonged to Sarai, the wife of Abram. Abram and Sarai had been promised a son who would become a great nation. Yet even a decade after the promise had been given, Sarai remained childless. In Sarai's attempt to "help God along a little" with His promise, she sent her slave girl, Hagar, into Abram's tent. The Bible says, "He slept with Hagar, and she conceived" (v. 4). Hagar, now pregnant with Abram's first son, began to run into trouble with her mistress.

Let's pick up the story in verses 5–6:

> Then Sarai said to Abram, "You are responsible for the wrong I am suffering. I put my servant in your arms, and now that she knows she is pregnant, she despises me. May the LORD judge between you and me."
>
> "Your servant is in your hands," Abram said. "Do with her whatever you think best." Then Sarai mistreated Hagar; so she fled from her.

And so Hagar ran away. That's what I would have done, too. That's what you and I do when we feel devalued or dishonored. We may not physically pack up and hit the road, but we do run away—emotionally and spiritually—from those who hurt us. Why do we run? The reasons are different for all of us. But most of us run to escape. We run to find a place where we might feel more significant or valued. Hagar ran to the wilderness to escape Sarai's abuse and the harshness of her circumstances.

Today, some of us run to anonymous relationships with fellow chatters on the Internet. Some run to bottles of pills or other destructive habits. Some run to the seemingly sanctimonious and sterilized escape hatch marked "Gossip." Oh yes, that's a place where we feel a temporary buzz of significance because we grow large in our own eyes as we belittle others. Think about where *you* run when you want to feel valuable. Think about where you end up. Is it really where you want to be? Does it satisfy your need to feel significant or honored?

At a Spring, in the Desert

As Hagar ran, she stopped to catch her breath by a spring of water in the wilderness. Can't you just see her? I'll bet she collapsed by the spring out of pure physical and emotional exhaustion. She felt like most of us do when we run—emotionally and spiritually spent. Many of us at different times in our lives have felt like Hagar must have felt—scared, resentful, tossed out, used. Those kinds of feelings can crush us, and we too can collapse under the weight. I wonder if Hagar wept from the pain of knowing that she'd never really been loved or valued. She had only been used and owned. I wonder if her tears were interrupted as she heard someone—someone as close as could be—speak her name.

"Hagar."

She'd heard her name spoken before, of course. Countless times. Perhaps in her youth, back in Egypt, before slavery, she'd heard her mother or father speak her name kindly. She'd certainly heard it spoken as a command, as Sarai sent her out to fetch water or gather some sticks for a fire. Had she heard Abram whisper her name as he embraced her in the tent…or did he even really know her name?

The voice she heard by the spring was different. Like no voice she had ever heard before. It was patient and kind and seemed to know her well. "Hagar, servant of Sarai, where have you come from, and where are you going?" (Genesis 16:8).

It was the voice of the angel of the Lord, whom many

scholars identify as the Lord Himself in angelic form. He found Hagar, spoke her name, and inquired of her. It was like He said, "Hagar, I see you. What are you doing here? What's going on?' She answered candidly, "I'm running away from my mistress Sarai" (v. 8).

The angel of the Lord told her to return to Sarai, but reassured her with a promise. "I will so increase your descendants that they will be too numerous to count" (v. 10).

Only God Himself could make such a promise. Not only did He see this broken young woman by the spring; He took note of her circumstances. Her pregnancy. Her relationships. Her dashed hopes. Her need for a hope and a future. I'll bet it had been a long, long time—if ever—since Hagar felt noticed or cared about. And now it was none other than the God of the universe who stooped low enough to see her, craned His neck just to hear her cry, and came to her as the angel of the Lord, just to speak her name. He not only knew her name; He also named her yet unborn son Ishmael, meaning "whom God hears."

It might have been the first time in her life that this insignificant female slave felt valued by someone. Not valued just because she was owned and "useful," but for who she was. "You are the God who sees me," she spoke back to the Lord (v. 13).

What an interesting way to characterize God. It should

startle our souls, just as it did Hagar's, when we realize that God truly sees us. Knows our circumstances. And genuinely cares.

Many of us feel like Hagar. Valued only because we are useful to someone else. Noticed only when someone needs something from us. But God sees you. God knows your name. He cares enough to inquire, "Where are you going? Where have you come from?" He speaks your name with tenderness, affection, and concern. He so values you that He, the great God, stoops low to find you, to touch you. As David noted, "Your right hand sustains me; you stoop down to make me great" (Psalm 18:35).

He sees you, just as He saw Hagar. He sees you even when you feel unnoticed or disregarded. And when His eyes look on you, you are bathed in honor. Psalm 62:7 reminds us that our honor is from God. "My salvation and my honor depend on God; he is my mighty rock, my refuge."

You see, your honor and value do not come from what you do or from others' opinions of you. You are honored because, just like Hagar, He has touched you with His presence, touched you with His promise, and touched you with His provision. You hold the attention of God. He heeds your heartache and finds you when you're exhausted. He sees you when you're broken, and you still hold a special place on the mantel of His heart.

FINGERPRINTS

A couple of years ago, I sat with my little Connor at the kitchen table as he pried the lids off his four new containers of Play-Doh. First red, then yellow, then green, and finally blue. Within seconds, the aroma of fresh Play-Doh filled the room...one of the happy fragrances of childhood. He pulled out each colorful mound, vigorously squeezing the dough between his fingers. Combining all four colors, he fashioned a creation that only a three-year-old architect could design. Finally, he gasped with awe and pride. "Mommy, it's *so beautiful!*"

"Tell me why it's so beautiful," I probed.

"I used all the colors," he answered, "then, I smushed it in my hands."

Since I thought he was finished describing his craftsmanship, I began to compliment his artwork. He quickly interrupted me. "But Mommy, it was my fingerprints that made it the most beautiful."

To me, as Connor's mother, anything that hosts his fingerprints is a work of art. But to the ordinary eye it must have looked like a misshapen blob of blended colors—poked and dented beyond any recognizable form, far more awkward looking than attractive. But, even so, as I felt his artwork with my fingers, it was beautiful to me.

Why was Connor's creation so compelling? For one reason: It looked a lot like you and me. We are a blending of the colors in our lives. Just like Hagar, we too have been poked, dented. We have been shaped and formed by the hands of a loving Creator whose eyes are always on us. Sometimes we've even felt the pressure of His gentle hands as He lovingly molds us. As we thumb through the photo album of our lives, we can't help but see His fingerprints.

When we felt enslaved, He touched us with His provision.

When we ran, He saw us and spoke to us.

When we were barren and hopeless, He gave us life and promise.

It is His touch on each frail form that makes us valuable. We all sometimes feel more awkward than attractive, but each of us has been marked with the loving and tender fingerprints of our Creator. And He sees something beautiful.

> For the LORD delights in his people; he crowns the humble with salvation. Let the faithful rejoice in this honor. Let them sing for joy as they lie on their beds.
>
> Psalm 149:4–5, NLT

TWO

A Touch of Intimacy

Touch is not only felt. Sometimes it is heard. Sometimes the deepest part of our soul can be touched only by melody and rhyme. It is often a simple love song that cuts through the din and clatter, allowing us to feel the unmistakable touch of the Lover of our souls.

I felt such a touch on one of the darkest days of my life.

And it came through a song.

It was early fall and early into my second pregnancy. All pregnancies are special, but this one seemed to carry with it extra hope—and even a bit of relief. This pregnancy was the culmination of five years of wishing, dreaming, praying, and trying to have another baby. We longed for another child to join our family. Our son, Clayton, had prayed for years that God would give him a baby brother.

So when we discovered in July of that same year that I was expecting, we all breathed a collective sigh of relief, quickly followed by thankfulness and excitement. Clayton immediately began to choose names and figure out how his furniture could be rearranged to accommodate his new miniature roommate! I was shopping for maternity clothes, trying not to throw up as I walked through my kitchen, and, of course, imagining this baby's high school and college graduation—and even his or her wedding! We hadn't experienced such giddy happiness as a family for years.

Then came the Tuesday morning in September when I discovered I was spotting. I immediately called the doctor's office. The nurse told me to lie down and that the doctor would call back soon. I did as the nurse instructed. Lying on my back, fear gripping my insides, I clasped the cordless phone with both hands and began to pray.

Just as I began to calm myself, the phone rang. I answered immediately, knowing it would be Dr. Trotter. It wasn't. It was my friend Genia, a pastor's wife in my town who had taken me under her spiritual wing. Just hearing her voice opened the floodgates. I began to weep and pour out my fears. "You be still and quiet," Genia told me, "while I pray." I don't remember what she prayed that September day—save one request. She asked our Father to "sing a new song over me."

Her request struck me—no one had ever prayed that for me before. We hung up and shortly after the doctor called and had me come in.

After an exam, the doctor told my husband and me that our little baby had no heartbeat. He explained the process of miscarriage and told me it would most likely take a couple of days. We were devastated. But we came home and continued to pray. The doctor's prediction proved true. My body was truly miscarrying.

Over the long days to follow, I felt such deep sadness. This loss was new and unfamiliar. I found no relief in spiritual supposition about God's will. I was grieving. Zora Neale Hurston put it this way: "I have been in sorrow's kitchen and licked out all the pots." I felt like I had, too. My spirit was aching, my soul was dry, and yet...something echoed down, down within a chamber of my heart.

It was a song.

Strangely, I had begun to hear its melody as I sat in Dr. Trotter's office, listening to the prognosis. It continued to take shape as I remained home, wishing and waiting. The melody grew and began to host lyrics in my mind. After several days, the doctor was not satisfied with my progress and called for a procedure to complete the process.

My husband and I met him in the hospital room where he began the procedure. What happened next defined for me how intimately God wants to touch our aching spirits.

I began to sing.

Before you dismiss this, you must understand that I *never* sing in intimate settings of just one or two. I never have. I don't sing to the radio in the car…I don't sing in the shower…I only sing if I'm totally alone or on stage with a microphone!

But on this day, I couldn't help but sing.

My spirit was destitute, and I could only respond to what I had heard over the past days. As tears streamed down my face, I sang back to God the song He had lovingly sung over me. He answered Genia's prayer on my behalf and showed me an intimate side of His character I had never seen, felt, or heard before.

Of Your mercy, I will sing.
Of Your mercy, I will sing.

With my mouth will I make known
 Your faithfulness to me
I will sing
 I will sing of your mercy.

You give me more than I could ever lose
 You do what's best for me
So I don't have to choose
 Within the heartache.
Your joy lets me turn loose
 So I can sing
And I will sing
 Of Your mercy.

As my frail voice lifted my Father's song back to Him, the nurse wiped the doctor's tears as they fell. Phil patted his own damp cheeks with tissue. Something happened that day in the hospital room that each of us experienced deeply, yet will always struggle to articulate.

For me, I felt the intimate, almost tangible touch of a Father who weeps when we weep, who comforts completely, and who makes His lyric and melody resonate hope within our despair.

Trying to explain to our young Clayton what had happened was terribly difficult also. After all, isn't God supposed to answer prayer? As I clumsily attempted to put our sorrow into words for Clay, I heard myself saying, "Son, some babies are born here on earth, but our baby was born in heaven."

It's the same with other areas of our lives as well. Things close to our hearts. Sometimes our deepest longings aren't born here on earth. Perhaps as you read this you are thinking about such a longing in your own heart. You feel that ache and long for a touch from heaven.

Our souls crave peace, hope, and intimacy. Yet some earthly longings can only be filled by heavenly provision. Some silences can only be filled by the intimacy of His song.

And some thirsts can only be quenched by living water.

A Woman, a Well, and a Wall

On the outskirts of a town called Sychar stood Jacob's well. Though many from the village drew from the well, one woman came there at an unlikely hour, in the heat of the day. We don't know her name, but Jesus knew her name and much more. He'd been walking for two and a half days, traveling from Judea to Galilee. As He journeyed through Samaria, He stopped to rest by the well while His disciples went into the city to buy food. "When a Samaritan woman came to draw water, Jesus said to her,

'Will you give me a drink?'" (John 4:7).

The woman must have been startled by His request. She responded, "'You are a Jew and I am a Samaritan woman. How can you ask me for a drink?' (For Jews do not associate with Samaritans)" (v. 9).

You see, it wasn't just a well that stood between Jesus and this woman. It was a wall. How could she ever feel the touch of Jesus on her life? Her harsh and hardened response to His simple request revealed a great deal about the gulf that separated them from one another that day.

The first issue was gender.

Women in ancient Hebrew culture weren't exactly what you'd call highly favored. In fact, they weren't favored at all. It was not uncommon to hear a Hebrew man praying with great relief and sincerity, "Lord, I thank You that I am not a woman." Rabbis proclaimed that "it is better to burn the law than to give it to a woman." The fact that Jesus chose to engage a woman in conversation was only the first crack in the wall that divided them.

The second issue was nationality.

This woman wasn't just a foreigner; she was (of all things!) a Samaritan. There was such animosity between Jews and Samaritans that it was said, "No Israelite is to eat of anything that is a Samaritan's, for it is as if he should eat swine's flesh." Samaritans were despised as worthless half-breeds and spiritually hollow opportunists.

No Orthodox Jew could stomach even setting foot on Samaritan turf. Rather than travel the easy route from Judea to Galilee, which goes through Samaria, the prejudiced Jews would add an extra few days to their journey by taking the desert route instead. When Jesus deliberately crossed the border into Samaria, He also crossed the barrier of hate—further chipping away at the wall of separation.

The third dividing issue was status.

Jesus was a rabbi. Rabbis were highly regarded and lived by a strict code of conduct. They were not permitted to speak publicly to any woman—not even their wives or sisters. But Jesus was hardly just a teacher of Law. He was both the Giver and the Fulfillment of the Law. At the well He taught that His authority was greater than that of the Law. And with this final blow, the wall of separation came tumbling down.

When you think about how high and forbidding that relational wall had been, you can understand more clearly how Jesus' words to her were like revolutionary arrows, piercing and shattering her cultural paradigm. She didn't know who this weary Jewish traveler was. His dialect and clothing may have clued her in that He was a rabbi. But even so, she had no idea with whom she spoke. And she had no idea how close she was to the touch of God upon her life.

Jesus said to her, "If you knew the gift of God and who it is that asks you for a drink, you would have asked him and he would have given you living water" (John 4:10). You see, Jesus knew what the woman did not. Jesus knew that *she* was the one who was truly thirsty. He knew she couldn't yet process that He was no ordinary Jew. That He was God wrapped in human clothing coming into her world.

"Though he was God," the apostle wrote, "he did not demand and cling to his rights as God. He made himself nothing; he took the humble position of a slave and appeared in human form" (Philippians 2:6–7, NLT). He broke through the boundaries of her preconceived notions and sat before her as a man, tired and thirsty, just so she could find relief for her arid soul. He became thirsty so she could have her thirst satisfied. Paul put it this way: "Though he was rich, yet for your sakes he became poor, so that you through his poverty might become rich" (2 Corinthians 8:9).

The woman hadn't yet grasped Jesus' comments because she was burdened by the weight of the empty water pot still in her hands. "'Sir,' the woman said, 'you have nothing to draw with and the well is deep. Where can you get this living water?'" (John 4:11).

I can't fault her for not tuning in more quickly. I spent many years just like her. I sought to fill deep eternal longings by dipping my leaky water jug into shallow wells.

Soap operas, romance novels, and shopping were all attempts at filling my longing for intimacy. I was trying to quench an intense, heavenly thirst with a few drops of tepid water. And it doesn't work. Maybe deep down the woman at Sychar knew this. I think deep down we all know this. We all know that within each of our souls is a craving, a longing, a burning desire to experience real intimacy.

Lots of us are so thirsty to be known that we dip into the rushing water of temporary satisfaction. Shallow relationships, low standards, promiscuity, compromise, and even outlandish behavior can all be buckets we dip into shallow water just to alleviate the intense craving even for a moment. The only problem is that those drinks are a bitter cup—which only leaves us more desperately thirsty.

Jesus says to us, just like He said to the woman, "Everyone who drinks this water will be thirsty again, but whoever drinks the water I give him will never thirst" (vv. 13–14).

How gently the words *never thirst* must have fallen—like soft rain on her parched soul. I wonder if her thoughts began to race. *How could someone never thirst? I know I'm always thirsty. But what is it I'm truly thirsty for? I've never really felt the thirst deep within me quenched. No one could do that, could he? Could He?*

Jesus interrupted her thoughts with this declaration: "Indeed, the water I give him will become in him a spring of water welling up to eternal life" (v. 14).

The woman simply replied, "Sir, give me this water" (v. 15).

I've tried to hear her voice as I've considered her words. Did she emphasize the word *give*? Was her inflection more intense on the word *me*? Or maybe she emphasized the word *this* as if no other water would do. Or did the weight of her emotion fall on the final word, *water,* as she pleaded? To me, this ordinary moment must have become extraordinary as she saw her thirst—and His provision—for the first time in her life.

The Thirst to Be Known

For just a moment let's leave Samaria. Let me take you to my basement in Springfield, Missouri. I want you to join me in the hallway that hosts our family photo gallery, for it's a place where I was reminded once again what real thirst looks like.

My friend Joey had spent the afternoon at our home with her husband, Mike, and their two children. After Joey packed up all the kid paraphernalia she sent Mike up with the kids to load the car. Our four-year-old son, Connor, and I were walking up with Joey when she noticed the photos lining the wall.

She first noticed our oldest son's photos. "He's grown so much!" she exclaimed. "He was such a *cute* baby!" While she went on for a bit about Clayton's pictures, little brother Connor began to pat her on the leg. At first, this went unnoticed. So he patted faster and harder. When she finally looked down at Connor, he was pointing up to his own baby pictures. "Look!" he said. "That's me! I am Connor!"

Joey instinctively knelt before him. "I know that you are Connor," she said and talked to him about his photos before we walked upstairs to say good-bye.

That ordinary hallway reminds me of the ordinary well in Sychar, because both Connor and the woman who drew at the well had the same thirst. It was the need, the thirst, to be truly known. Jesus knew what would quench her thirst, and He wanted her to know it, too. That's why He said, "Go, call your husband and come back" (v. 16). She must have felt the sting of her dry soul when she confessed her shame to Him. "I have no husband," she replied (v. 17).

Jesus continued, "You are right when you say you have no husband. The fact is, you have had five husbands, and the man you now have is not your husband. What you have just said is quite true" (v. 18).

This woman must have really felt exposed. All those

men...husbands, lovers, and men she'd known. But until this moment, she had never known a man who really knew *her.* In a sense, through so many men, she was patting and pointing and saying, "That's me. I am a woman...know me."

We all have the thirst to be known. It is one of our most basic longings. To be intimately connected with another, vulnerable and exposed yet still embraced and accepted, has to be one of the greatest cravings of the human soul.

The woman recognized by now that she was not speaking to any ordinary Jewish rabbi, so she said to Him, "'I know that Messiah' (called Christ) 'is coming. When he comes, he will explain everything to us'" (v. 25). What Jesus said next is the most marvelous part of the story. "I who speak to you am he" (v. 26). If I had been at that well on that day, if I had been that woman, I would have become weak in the knees! I would have felt time stand still. Even today I can't wrap my mind around what happened at that well. Jesus knew her and wanted her to know Him.

Think of it! At this point, He had not yet revealed Himself—even to His closest followers—with such a definitive, authoritative statement. I think that in the kind heart of God, He had reserved the moment of such an intimate revelation for *this* woman.

A sexually loose Samaritan woman.

Amazing!

As if to say, "There is no one whom I deem unworthy of My intimate touch. I want to know you. You, who are stained and ordinary. I want to meet you at your well and satisfy you. I want you to know Me, too. I will reveal Myself to you in truth and intimacy, if you just linger at the well long enough to listen and inquire of Me. Your longings are great, but My supply is greater. Let Me fill your cup and touch you with tender intimacy."

WHAT CAN WE DRAW FROM THE WELL?

God may choose to step into our lives at unusual times, in unusual ways. Perhaps even as you read the words on this page. Right in the middle of the gray, ordinary routine of life, in those times when we feel least "worthy" or "spiritual," we may suddenly experience the startling nearness of the Lord who loves us.

That's what happened to the woman at the well, under the hot middle-eastern sun on "just another day" in Sychar. It wasn't a worship center with stained glass windows where she met Jesus and felt His touch. It wasn't some mountaintop retreat center under a full moon.

No, it was at the village well. It was right in the midst of her daily routine that God stepped in and made her ordinary extraordinary. I have a feeling that when Jesus Christ suddenly appeared in that woman's humdrum, everyday schedule, that well *did* become a worship center!

God seeks to do the same for you and me. In the course of our everyday lives, He steps in, intrigues us, exposes our need, and reveals Himself to us. He told the Samaritan woman, "If you knew the gift of God and who it is that asks you for a drink, you would have asked him and he would have given you living water" (v. 10).

Lady, if you only knew! If you only realized—for even a moment—just Who it is you're talking to!

It took her a while to realize the gift that came to her on that day of divine visitation. Perhaps she missed it at first because He was packaged as a thirsty, tired Jewish traveler.

We miss His visitations, too...and for similar reasons. We fail to see His fingerprints on the events of our lives. We fail to praise Him for those amazing "coincidences" that bring grace and help and blessing into our days. We fail to recognize His still, small voice that whispers tender truth to us and counsels us in the midst of our routines and in the crush of our trials and heartaches. Sometimes it's the encouragement of a friend or the lyrics of a song that finds us at the well and reminds us that God knows us. What a gracious Lord who interrupts our ordinary moments with such extraordinary creativity and care.

So *look* for Him at the well of your routines. *Seek* Him in the "dailyness" of life. Remember His words to the prophet: "You will seek me and find me when you seek me with all your heart. I will be found by you" (Jeremiah 29:13–14).

Don't reserve your day of visitation for Sunday alone. He seeks to touch you with His tender, knowing touch wherever you are. He will find you behind your computer screen, changing a diaper, driving a car pool, or cooking a meal. (He even shows up in the midst of that endless pile of laundry!) When you recognize the gift of God that touches you, your well will become a worship center, too.

ONE WOMAN...IN THE MIDST OF MILLIONS

Yolanda had plans for Friday night that none of her friends knew about. She was tired of the routine of life, weary from the rejection she felt, and emptied by the harsh realities she couldn't change. Her own family had rejected her. In fact, her pictures had been removed from the living room walls. She was disowned, dead in her mother's eyes. The pain of her life seemed stronger than her faith, so on Friday night she planned to use the bottle of sleeping pills she had been hiding in her drawer.

Her friends, however, began to pester her to go to a prison on Friday with the campus ministry group. She continually told them no, for she was determined to follow through with her plans. Finally, they wore her down, and she decided to go. *After all,* she thought, *I can take the pills when I get back*. So off she went.

During the prison service, she felt completely unmoved. Cold as stone. Some of the antics during the service were irritating, and she kept a keen eye on her watch, waiting to head home.

Near the end of the meeting, an older, balding man with gray hair, silver glasses, and a blue denim work shirt approached her. "Miss," he said, "I have a word for you. It's in Isaiah 49:15." Yolanda looked down at her open Bible and quickly turned to the passage. "Can a mother forget the baby at her breast and have no compassion on the child she has borne? Though she may forget, I will not forget you!"

How could he have known?

Yolanda burst into tears and looked up to thank the prophetic stranger. But no one was there. Her eyes darted quickly around the locked and secured room. No one fit the description of the man who visited her. He simply wasn't there. With growing certainty—and awe—Yolanda realized she had been visited by One who was not a stranger. One who was intimately acquainted with her. One who knew her heartache, knew her secret thoughts, and had visited her and touched her with truth.

Yolanda had made plans to alleviate her pain…but God had other plans for her. Plans for life. Plans for hope. Plans for a future.

> "I know the plans I have for you," declares the LORD, "plans to prosper you and not to harm you, plans to give you hope and a future."
>
> JEREMIAH 29:11

Yolanda knew the tender touch of a Father who came to her when she needed Him most. She knew how His touch filled every longing to be accepted and whole. She is a reflection of the intimate touch of a Father who said, "Never will I leave you; never will I forsake you" (Hebrews 13:5). Just like the woman at the well, Yolanda mattered deeply to God. He came to her when her life was in peril, and in the midst of crowds and confusion, He touched her with the certainty that He knew her well. He knew her heartache and her thoughts of self-destruction. He also knew the hope and future that only He could bring.

God seeks you too in this crowded, often impersonal world of ours. He seeks you in the midst of the millions just so He can reveal Himself to you. Do you see Him in the crowd, or do you miss Him because you are so focused on your own plans? The woman in Sychar had plans also. They were simple: fulfill daily obligations and fill her water jug.

Let's return to that well just in time to see the disciples returning with food for Jesus. By this time, the woman's plans and future had utterly changed. "Then, leaving her water jar, the woman went back to the town and said to the people, 'Come, see a man who told me everything I ever did'" (John 4:28–29). She left a meaningless, empty water jug by the well because, for the first time, she had tasted *living* water. She had been invited to know the God who knew her—and now she went to invite others to know Him, too.

Are you willing to leave your water jug behind and be filled only by the water Jesus gives?

TOUCHED WITH THE KNOWLEDGE OF GOD

The most intimate moment at the well may have been when Jesus' and the woman's eyes met, as He spoke the words: "I who speak to you am he" (John 4:26).

There is no more intimate touch you and I can receive than to be in communion with Jesus and to have Him reveal Himself to us. His invitation is clear. "Come to me, all you who are weary and burdened, and I will give you rest. Take my yoke upon you and learn from me, for I am gentle and humble in heart, and you will find rest for your souls" (Matthew 11:28–29).

Only intimacy with Him fills our longings. It not only satisfies us, but it brings satisfaction to the heart of God. Do you remember what Jesus said to His disciples when they brought food to Him? "I have food to eat that you know nothing about" (John 4:32).

You see, Jesus too was satisfied. His intimate exchange was more gratifying than mere food. He came to seek and save what was lost. He came to fill our emptiness with life abundant. He came to lead us to springs of living water (Revelation 7:17). He came to amaze us with the gracious words from His lips (Luke 4:22). He came to quiet us with His love as He rejoices over us with singing (Zephaniah 3:17). He came to draw us near when we were far away (Ephesians 2:13). Just as with the woman at the well, He longs to draw you close, so you can feel His touch and hear His voice. He longs to sing hope over you through the moments of your days, whether they are commonplace or catastrophic.

About six months after our second child was born in

heaven, we discovered we were again expecting. You guessed it…Connor! On December 9, 1998, God allowed our third baby to be born here on earth! If you knew little Connor, you'd understand why…he's a wonderful, wide-eyed wild man. Heaven isn't quite ready for him yet! He needs some time here on earth to work out the kinks and get redemption! You and I also need time here on this side of eternity where we can stand in sorrow's kitchen and hear the sweet music of our Father orchestrate hope within the despair.

We all need time here to linger at the well so we can be interrupted, exposed, and drawn into the presence of the living God. The apostle Paul reminds us that right now we do see through a glass dimly, but when we see Him face-to-face we will know fully, even as we are fully known (1 Corinthians 13:12). Until then, God gives us time to taste the bitterness of loss, to feel the emptiness of our water jug, and to find the complete satisfaction of knowing Him and being known by Him.

So welcome Him to your well. Linger there and listen to Him. Once you have felt the intimate touch of Jesus, your deepest longings will be satisfied.

THREE

His Sheltering Embrace

It was Thursday night. I'd had a long day of writing, and my brain was practically evaporating away! Since I know how dangerous I can be in the kitchen on nights like these, my husband and I decided to load up our two sons and the babysitter and go out to dinner.

As we stood in line to order, our youngest son, Connor, started getting fussy, wanting me to hold him. Our sitter, Helen, had been standing behind me, so I turned and handed her my purse.

"Hold this," I said. "I've got to hold the baby." She

didn't answer but took the purse.

Clayton, who was eleven at the time, quickly approached to walk me to our table. After we were seated, Helen handed me my purse.

"Thanks for taking it from me," I said. "I just couldn't manage."

"I *didn't* take it from you," she said sheepishly. "You handed it to some lady."

"What!?"

Helen giggled. "She looked pretty shocked, but took it anyway. I went to her and took it back. I think she was a little confused!"

Clayton groaned. "Mom," he pleaded, "please pull out your cane so she'll know you're blind, not crazy."

I acted like a grown-up and laughed, casually dismissing my blunder. But on the inside, I was mortified. *What must that woman think of me? I don't look blind, so she really must think I'm crazy. What must Helen think? I look so stupid right now.*

I realized I was so upset because I cared deeply about how I looked to others. Here I was, eating out with my family, trying not to draw attention to myself, and I pull a stunt like that! My ego was bruised. I felt humiliated, and deep down I didn't want to laugh at all. I wanted to hide! And guess what? God wanted me to hide, too.

In fact, He wants us all to hide...in Him.

HIDDEN IN HIM

Several years ago our boys splashed in the ocean of Gulf Shores, Alabama. I think our two-year-old must have consumed his weight in beach sand that day. We hadn't been there long when Clayton ran to me exclaiming, "Mom, hold this for me! It's the tiniest shell I've ever seen!"

He pleaded with me to protect his newest treasure. I consented and opened my hand. The shell was smaller than my smallest fingerprint. It was so tiny that it was barely detectable in the palm of my hand. Even so, I pressed it between my thumb and index finger. Since Clayton was my treasure, I would guard his treasure with diligence.

I settled in my beach chair, digging my toes into the warm sand. The afternoon passed slowly, as time on the beach often does. The winds shifted along with the tide, but I was immovable! I was queen of the beach—cemented to my throne with sunscreen and sweat.

Without notice, it hit! I may not have moved, but the *shoreline* did. A giant wave had encroached upon my sovereign domain, immersing me in a flood of ocean water! Sprinkled, dipped, and dunked—I was baptized by *all* denominational standards!

But what about my son's treasure? Cautiously, I

peeled back my clenched fingers to see if the shell had made it through my drenching…or returned to the sea. Ah, there it was! I could still feel it, secure in a mother's grip. I'd done it! My son would never know the peril of this single loving act! I was proud. I felt like a *real* mom—the kind of mother June Cleaver only dreamed of being.

After a while, Clayton ran up to me, breathless. "Mom," he gasped, "do you still have my shell?" "Yes," I proudly replied, and recounted my heroism to him. He simply giggled, "Thanks, Mom," and ran back into the waves.

My thoughts shifted from my soaked head to bigger things. Like how tiny that shell felt in my hand—and how tiny we are in God's great hand. As His precious treasure, we are tucked within His care. Jesus told His disciples:

> "My sheep recognize my voice and I know who they are. They follow me and I give them eternal life. They will never die and no one can snatch them out of my hand. My Father, who has given them to me, is greater than all. And no one can snatch anything out of the Father's hand. I and the Father are One."
>
> JOHN 10:27–30, PHILLIPS

No one can snatch anything out of the Father's hand. When it comes to His children, God's touch is more than a caress—it's a firm grip. In those times when storms roar into our lives and we feel we might be swept away in a flood of anxiety and heartache, He is the one who tenderly shields our souls. His hand is the place of ultimate security and refuge. Our Father holds on to us with tenacity and graces us with tenderness. It's mind-boggling to think we are actually hidden in Him.

That thought caused David to shake his head in wonder, too. In Psalm 32:7, he wrote:

> You are my hiding place;
> you...surround me with songs of deliverance.

In the New Testament, Paul affirms that as believers, our "life is now hidden with Christ in God" (Colossians 3:3). When we hide in Him, we are covered and comforted by Him. *In Him* is a great place to be! Where better?

I find myself often needing to hide in Him. For when I do, I feel His sheltering touch. And let's face it, sometimes the wind blows hard and storms erupt suddenly. Those waves come crashing down on us out of nowhere. It's much safer to be securely nestled in His hand than it is to run to Him when the dark clouds roll in and the lightning flashes.

Again, David writes:

> God is our refuge and strength,
> an ever-present help in trouble.
> Therefore we will not fear, though the earth give way
> and the mountains fall into the heart of the sea,
> though its waters roar and foam
> and the mountains quake with their surging.
>
> Psalm 46:1–3

He is our refuge.

We find our comfort in the assurance that He does hide us in His hand. And He is there when we need Him most.

Safe in His Arms

Preena knew what it felt like to be rescued by the sheltering arms of Jesus. Since the death of her father when she was two, she had lived in an Indian Hindu temple. Her mother had sold her for fifty rupees to be a temple child, and the centuries-old solid rock temple was her entire world. The walls and towers on the grounds were covered with hideous and barbaric figures.

Each day, as Preena fulfilled her temple duties, she passed by grotesque depictions of Hindu gods. There was the goddess Kali, with a headdress made of snakes, standing upon the stone body of a child. In one hand she held a sword; in the other, a bloody human head. The temple grounds also hosted a statue depicting the cruel goddess Sheva. She held a pitchfork in one hand and in the other a helpless child.

Preena's world was frightening and cruel. By the age of seven she had been branded and abused and was to be married to one of the many brutal and merciless Hindu gods. She struggled within the hopeless darkness of her young existence and longed to be safe.

One night, as Preena lay on her sleeping mat among the other temple girls, she overheard the whispers of two temple women. "...A white woman, one of those Christian missionaries," hissed one of the priestesses. "Her name is Amy and she steals children from the temples. Once she even dyed her skin brown and sneaked into the temple. She has strong powers from her God, whom they call the Lord Jesus Christ."

"Filthy Christians!" the other woman spat.

Preena hadn't heard much. But what she had heard started echoes of wonder within her soul. *"Amy...child stealer...the Lord Jesus Christ."*

Perhaps the Lord Jesus Christ really does *have great power,* Preena mused. *Maybe this Amy would steal* me. With these thoughts, a door of hope began to crack open, letting just a glimmer of light into Preena's dark despair.

Soon after, the literal door of her temple prison was accidentally left cracked open. For years, she had been watching for such an opportunity. With all the courage she could muster, she slipped secretly out of the unlocked door one dark evening.

With bare brown feet pounding against packed dirt roads, she ran toward the shelter she barely understood. Dashing toward the edge of the village, she splashed across a shallow stream. Bewildered, she made her way through a grove of palms and into a neighboring village.

She was spotted by an old woman as she ran. "Child!" the woman barked. "Where are you going?"

"I'm looking for the child-stealing Amy," Preena replied. As the villagers gathered around Preena, they recognized her clothes as belonging to a temple girl. Since a slave of the gods was never to run away, the faithful Hindu worshippers began to chase her to return her to the temple.

Shouts, threatening faces, and harsh hands surrounded Preena. Gasping, she whirled around and fled in utter panic. She turned down an obscure village street when suddenly a woman stepped out of a door in front of her. Preena stopped in her tracks—it was a white woman! Could this be the child stealer she was looking for?

What happens next in the story displays our God's sheltering touch. "Help me!" shrieked Preena as she hurled herself into the white woman's arms. "I don't want to be a slave of the gods. I want the Lord Jesus Christ!" The white woman's arms tightened around Preena, shielding her from her angry pursuers.

The crowd began to shout, "She belongs to the temple! She has run away!" By this time the temple women had arrived, laden with glittering jewels around their necks and arms. Their eyes also glistened with a bitter and cold cruelty. "She is ours!" they screamed. "We paid fifty rupees for that child!"

But the white missionary would not open her protective arms. With unyielding defiance she refused to let the trembling Preena go. Instead, she paid the temple women fifty rupees, buying Preena's freedom.

For the first time in her brief life, Preena was safe. She clung to the missionary named Amy as she was led gently into her new home. Amy Carmichael sheltered thousands of Indian children over her many years as a missionary to India.[1]

What Amy Carmichael did for Preena is what God does for you and me. He is the shelter we run to. He

---

1. Mildred A. Martin, *Missionary Stories with the Millers* (Green Pastures Press: Mifflin, TN, 1993), 130–6.

envelops us with His love. He even buys us back. When we are being pursued, He sweeps us up into His safe and secure arms. The Lord Jesus Christ Himself is our shelter. When we are being accused or pursued, He becomes the strong tower to which we can run.

CITIES OF REFUGE

In ancient cities, walls were erected to provide protection against enemy invaders. Because of the fortified walls, the city enjoyed a measure of peace and security. Nothing short of a determined assault by a powerful enemy could harm them.

Though all ancient cities were walled, certain Hebrew cities were designated as "Cities of Refuge." When God divvied up the Promised Land between the tribes of His chosen people, He gave the Levites forty-eight towns. Six of those towns were designated by God to be Cities of Refuge. These cities were to be places where anyone could flee for safety from unjust accusation.

God told Moses to "select some towns to be your cities of refuge, to which a person who has killed someone accidentally may flee. They will be places of refuge from the avenger, so that a person accused of murder may not die before he stands trial before the assembly" (Numbers 35:11–12). In other words, even though these were

Hebrew cities, their gates were open to anyone who needed their safety. Verse 15 mentions that "Israelites, aliens and any other people living among them" could find shelter there. In fact, highways and bridges were built to provide easy access to these particular cities.

Cities of refuge are a picture of our fortress of salvation. Psalm 28:8 tells us, "The LORD is the strength of his people, a fortress of salvation for his anointed one." God made a place for us when we were needy and accused by giving us access to Himself. Just as the Cities of Refuge invited all into their gates (Numbers 35:15), so God does the same for us.

We all need a city of refuge because we all stand accused by our enemy. In the book of Revelation, we are reminded that Satan is called "the accuser of our brothers, who accuses them before our God day and night" (12:10). He is a fierce and persistent foe who never tires of the battle. His accusations and attacks are personal—and always below the belt!

You and I can easily grow weary in this war. We become fatigued and worn down by the constant onslaught of lies and venomous condemnation. We need a place to hide from the fiery darts and someone to defend our honor and preserve our lives. Thankfully, we have a safe place in our High Priest, Jesus. He is the One who conquered our enemy and ever lives to make intercession for us.

If you need a refuge, listen to the words of Jesus: "The one who comes to Me I will by no means cast out" (John 6:37, NKJV). Just like Preena, we can flee "for refuge to lay hold of the hope set before us" (Hebrews 6:18, NKJV). We can find our comfort in knowing that our Father will always be our refuge. When we run to Him, He scoops us up into His arms. He fortifies us. He becomes our Rock of salvation. Strong. Stable. Secure.

We often try to be a rock of stability within ourselves, but our strength is eroded by the merciless tide of demands that wash over us. Sometimes the reason we feel so overwhelmed, however, is not simply because of our schedules and the stresses of life. No, sometimes we feel overwhelmed because we run to the wrong rock for shelter.

THE ROCK OF REFUGE

Part of the lie we believe is that *we* are a rock. When life is demanding and the stresses scrape against our souls, we misguidedly believe that we should fortify ourselves and draw from some inner reservoir of our own strength. Not so! Consider what the psalmist said: "From the end of the earth I will cry to You, when my heart is overwhelmed; Lead me to the rock that is higher than I" (Psalm 61:2, NKJV). You see, you and I can be a rock, but compared to

THE Rock, we're just tiny pebbles! In and of ourselves, we are not designed to weather the storm. Left to ourselves, we will drown in the tidal waves and be tossed by the wind.

But there is a Rock that is higher.

We must trade in our tiny strength (which is really weakness) for the fortitude found only in the Immovable Rock. We must hide our weary souls in the cleft of His rock.

I am not ashamed to say that I *need* the Rock that is higher than me. He grounds me, centers me, and keeps me.

Early in ministry, I was asked to do a benefit concert for Child Evangelism Fellowship. For months, I went from church to church in Tallahassee, Florida, singing and recruiting local kids to come sing with me for the big night. By the evening of the concert, we had just over a hundred kids. The auditorium was full of proud parents and curious onlookers.

Music blared from the sound system as kids streamed from all the doors to join me on stage. It was electric! We sang several songs, and then the kids went to sit with their folks as I finished up the remainder of the concert. I began to play the keyboard as they were seating themselves.

The longer I played and with every chord, the worse

the sound became. I instinctively lifted my foot from the sustain pedal to quiet the dissonant sound now echoing throughout the sanctuary. But it made no difference! I tapped my sustain pedal with rhythmic precision, but there was no relief! Evidently the sustain mechanism in my keyboard had malfunctioned. The five chords I had just played were still vibrating through the building, sounding more like a haunted house than a Christian concert.

This was a terrible thing. Fear and humiliation coursed like ice water through my veins. I wanted someone brilliant to run onto the stage and say, "Here, I'll take care of it." But, of course, no one did. In those few seconds that felt like centuries, I weighed my options and decided to shut off the keyboard. I made a quick comment to the crowd. "I bet you thought only musicians were temperamental. Evidently, so are musical instruments!"

The crowd exhaled a collective sound of relieved laughter as I reached back and turned the power off! I assumed this would clear the program and we would start again. Then I turned it back on and began to play again. One chord, two chords, three chords...yikes! It was *not* fixed! I immediately repeated the routine, tapping the pedal, then powering off the uncooperative keyboard. I was reeling inside.

I needed the keyboard to finish the concert, but it was

now time for Plan B. I tried to maintain composure, but inside I was totally undone. I felt alone on that stage, with an unfixable problem. Then I had a brilliant thought… *I'll use the piano!* I called my companion to come up and walk me back to the piano, awkwardly placed near the back of the stage behind a modesty rail. Seating myself on the piano bench as the sound tech set up a boom stand, I was now ready for Plan B to slide flawlessly into place.

Carefully removing the mike from the boom, I stood in front of the piano to say a word before I sat to play. As I began to speak, I gingerly laid my hand on the top beam of the half-wall modesty rail. No sooner had I done this, than the railing that extended the entire length of the stage collapsed forward, sending mammoth echoes through the auditorium. The only thing louder than the sound of the wall crashing against the floor was the panicked sound of the helpless audience gasping and squealing.

That was it! I wanted to bail! I felt so desperate and helpless. More than anything I wanted to walk off that stage and never return. But twenty long minutes of misery remained.

What happened at that moment—in those split seconds—has always fascinated me. I had an overwhelming urge to call my dad. I imagined him running up onto the stage and lifting the railing back into place. I imagined hearing him whisper, "It's okay, Jenna. I'll take care of this."

My dad wasn't at the concert, but the memory and reality of my dad was forever embedded in my heart. He was always my rescuer and my shelter. His touch could fix anything—broken toys, broken promises, and broken hearts. In my moment of vulnerability and desperation, it was his touch that I longed for. I knew that if he were there, this would have all been okay because my dad could fix anything.

Though you may have never known a dad like that, you do have such a Father. He comes to you when you feel weak and alone. It is His touch that lifts the fallen walls of your hopes and dreams. His arms surround you; they envelop you, and His unseen hands can fix anything broken in your life. If you feel your world beginning to crumble, He becomes your strength. When you feel exposed and vulnerable, He becomes your refuge. Your shelter. Your hiding place.

And He will never, never let you go.

> The LORD has become my fortress,
> and my God the rock in whom I take refuge.
>
> PSALM 94:22

FOUR

The Hand That Guides

Standing in the Radiant Bookstore one cold December afternoon, I met a gentleman named Rosario. His voice smiled as he introduced himself. His companion reached for my hand and placed it on Rosario's hand as he spoke.

Rosario, you see, is blind. Like me.

In order for us to orient ourselves to one another, we bridged the gap of sight with touch. As we stood speaking as old friends who had just met, we never pulled our hands away from one another. At times, we would shake them or grip a little tighter. During tender times of our conversation, I would place my remaining hand on our grip. But until our conversation ended, the touch lingered. It was the physical bond that reassured each of us that the other was still there.

Somehow, in the darkness, touch is the reassuring affirmation that we are not alone. Touch grounds us, guides us, and orients us.

When my world became dark as a fifteen-year-old girl, my greatest challenge was to remain oriented. I had to find a way to navigate my new darkness—physically, spiritually, and emotionally.

For physical orientation I relied heavily on the guiding touch of my dad.

He was the one I felt most secure with. His hand was always steady, his touch gentle, and his pace was perfect for me. The emotional and spiritual darkness that blindness invited, however, was far more difficult to navigate.

Isn't that the nature of hardship? Sometimes it isn't the event itself that leaves us dazed and confused, as much as the trappings and wrappings that surround it. Blindness is one thing, but having to reconcile why God doesn't heal is another kind of darkness. Coping with deteriorated retinas is challenging enough; fighting the anger, disappointment, and bitterness resulting from that loss is another matter altogether.

You know what I mean.

The emotional and spiritual shadows that loom over us can completely disorient us. We lose sight of where we're going, where we've been, and even who we are. Most sadly, we lose sight of God.

That's when life gets really frightening. In the darkness and pain of personal crises, we *must* have the touch of our unseen Father to keep us oriented. At times we may sense His affectionate pat on the hand. At other times, He grasps us a little more tightly so we're sure He won't leave.

You don't have to be in total darkness to become disoriented. I know many folks who are fully sighted—yet are as confused and bewildered as they can be. Their disorientation is of a far more serious strain.

It is spiritual.

Spiritual disorientation results in questionable actions, wavering beliefs, and devastating consequences. It leads us through a maze of confusion and lands us at destinations we would never have chosen. The hard truth is, we simply *can't* find our way back to the right road, the right path, the right place, the right life...apart from the Father bridging the darkness and making contact in our lives. The touch of His hand becomes our compass.

This isn't anything new for God. He's touched the lives of men and women since the beginning of everything.

He's touched prophets who became disoriented by their own rebellion. He's touched kings who had a less than stellar track record. And He's even touched the ungodly who cried out in desperation for guidance. The hand of the Lord is neither slow nor selective. He will touch any who recognize their own darkness and need the pressure of His hand to guide them.

He's done it for me.

He has not yet touched my physical eyes so I can see, but He has enlightened "the eyes of [my] heart" (Ephesians 1:18). He has touched my fragile feelings and given me truth as my fortress. He has touched my ashes and made them beautiful. His touch has oriented me and guided me, and I know He longs to touch you, too. When you realize what His touch can do, you will call on Him just like I did.

And just like Jonah did.

Running into Darkness

Open up the car door and let me out most anywhere in the world, and you will have one disoriented lady. Without physical sight, without someone to guide me, I would have no idea which way to turn.

There's nothing amazing about that. It's what you would expect. What's amazing to me is how quickly and how completely we can lose our spiritual bearings when we're disobedient to the Lord or reject His counsel and guidance. The confusion rolls in like fog off the bay, and the darkness is profound.

I can't think of a better example than a prophet named Jonah. By deliberately turning his back on God, he ran into a darkness beyond what most of us could even imagine.

Now brace yourself. This is not a fish story—this is a story about you and me and how God mercifully intervenes, pulls us from darkness that swallows us, and sets our feet back on the path of His purpose.

Jonah was a prophet from Galilee whom God called to go to Nineveh and preach repentance. The fact that Nineveh was the capital of the Assyrian empire made this something of a tall order. Merciless, aggressive, and brutal, the Assyrians were constantly laying siege upon Israel. For years, Jonah had watched his countrymen taken away as slaves, women and children killed, and his beloved land stolen. *How could he possibly go to Nineveh and give those evil heathens a chance to repent? Why didn't God just FRY them, as they so richly deserved?*

Who can explain or comprehend God's heart of compassion? It didn't make sense to Jonah, and he didn't want to go. I wouldn't have wanted to go either. Let's just say Jonah came up short in the obedience department and refused to accept God's will for his life. So he ran in the opposite direction. He hurried to the nearest seaport and booked passage on a ship heading toward Tarshish, at the edge of the civilized world.

You might find it amusing that the name Jonah means "a dove." I'd say that's pretty appropriate, since he flew the coop! He spread his wings and flew into the wrong blue yonder. But even when we begin to slip off the path and get lost in oblivion, God never loses track of us. Not for an instant. He knew how and where to find Jonah, just as He knows how and where to find you and me.

Somewhere in the middle of Jonah's journey in the wrong direction, a monster storm descended on the ship.

Storms don't intimidate God. He has no trouble finding His way through the dark clouds, lashing rain, and wild wind. The Bible says,

> The LORD has His way
> In the whirlwind and in the storm,
> And the clouds are the dust of His feet.
>
> NAHUM 1:3, NKJV

Not so for us frail, earthbound creatures. It's amazing how a storm can awaken us to the reality of how lost we really are. Jonah had become tangled in the vine of rebellion, and now it was time to taste the fruit. Unfortunately, the fruit of rebellion is always death. When Jonah cast himself into the ocean (knowing full well that he was the cause of all the trouble), that's how the story should have ended. Right? After all, that would have been fair. I'm so thankful that our God is "unfair" when it comes to our rebellion and sin. "He does not treat us as our sins deserve or repay us according to our iniquities" (Psalm 103:10). He swallows us up in His mercy when we are sinking in sin, just as He did for His reluctant prophet.

For Jonah, mercy was a giant mackerel with a man-sized appetite! Now let me remind you, this is a nonfiction book...Jonah really was swallowed by a great fish. In fact, there are actually half a dozen documented accounts of humans surviving being swallowed by large fish. Even though it's incredible to imagine, it is credible! Jesus Himself spoke of the prophet and the incident with the fish as historical fact (Matthew 12:39–41; Luke 11:30–32).

Now picture Jonah. When he plunged into the cold waves of that churning sea, he expected to drown. He imagined the end would come rather quickly. It would be unpleasant, and then it would be over. But somehow, it didn't happen that way. What was going on? Was he alive or dead? Even if he was alive, he didn't expect it to last long. He had seaweed wrapped around his head and neck, and he could feel his life ebbing away. At that point, he didn't even know up from down—literally and figuratively. Talk about disoriented!

When it's that uncertain and dark, you feel sheer terror. But even in Jonah's blackest moment, it was a light inside that began to orient him. The Bible actually records Jonah's prayer in that dreadful place. Throughout the pages of Scripture, you will encounter all kinds of prayers on all kinds of occasions in all kinds of places. But this has to be the first recorded prayer from *under* the Mediterranean.

> From inside the fish Jonah prayed to the LORD his God. He said:
>
> "In my distress I called to the LORD, and he answered me. From the depths of the grave I called for help, and you listened to my cry. You hurled me into the deep, into the very heart of the seas, and the currents swirled about me; all your waves and breakers swept over me. I said, 'I have been banished from your sight; yet I will look again toward your holy temple.' The engulfing waters threatened me, the deep surrounded me; seaweed was wrapped around my head. To the roots of the mountains I sank down; the earth beneath barred me in forever. But you brought my life up from the pit, O LORD my God.
>
> "When my life was ebbing away, I remem-

bered you, LORD, and my prayer rose to you, to your holy temple.

"Those who cling to worthless idols forfeit the grace that could be theirs. But I, with a song of thanksgiving, will sacrifice to you. What I have vowed I will make good. Salvation comes from the LORD."

And the LORD commanded the fish, and it vomited Jonah onto dry land.

Jonah 2

Did you know that Jonah's prayer is really a series of quotations from Psalms? In that dark and confining place, with death pressing in, the disobedient prophet began to quote his favorite psalms from memory. You see, even in deep disorientation, His Word will be a lamp unto our feet and a light unto our path. What some would call fish guts, Jonah called a prayer closet! He must have knelt among the catch of the day and glimpsed the goodness of God.

"Those who cling to worthless idols forfeit the grace that could be theirs. But I, with a song of thanksgiving, will sacrifice to you. What I have vowed I will make good" (vv. 8–9). The prophet shifted his gaze from his problem to his Provider. He became thankful for his holy life preserver, which God had mercifully prepared.

Now consider: Jonah prayed these psalms to God with no idea that God would provide a way out. For all he knew, he was about to be digested. I wonder what he was thinking. As a prophet of Jehovah, certainly he could have memorized many psalms. Why did he choose these? Maybe it's because when life is slipping away, what really matters rises to the surface. What Jonah thought about in the darkness was how thankful he was for his relationship with the living God and how desperate he was for God's deliverance. Jonah cast himself upon the mercy of God as he prayed, "I have been banished from your sight; yet I will look again toward your holy temple" (v. 4).

I love that verse, because poor Jonah didn't even know which way was up, much less in which direction to look for God's holy temple. But he knew in his heart what his eyes couldn't see. He knew he could fix his gaze on God and find his way again. Sometime after Jonah spoke to God, God spoke to the fish. "And the LORD commanded the fish, and it vomited Jonah onto dry land" (v. 10).

Now Jonah—the disheveled, fishy smelling, possibly bleached-skinned prophet—made the journey into Nineveh. From wherever Jonah hit the beach, he had at least four hundred inland miles to travel to reach the capital of Assyria...which would have given him lots of time to think. I wonder if he contemplated the kind heart of God, not only to the Ninevites, but toward himself as well. I wonder if he glanced down at his bleached arms and hands and quoted, "O LORD God Almighty, who is like you? You are mighty, O LORD, and your faithfulness surrounds you" (Psalm 89:8).

Jonah became disoriented by his own rebellion, yet with one glance toward God's holy hill he became oriented again, and God restored him to his original purpose. How encouraging! I can't help but be reminded of the words of James: "Come near to God and he will come near to you" (James 4:8). God is always willing to touch us. But we must be willing to overcome our own pride and humble ourselves before Him so we can receive His touch.

When we rebel against God's plan, we thwart His purpose for our lives. We must therefore be careful how we walk. We must listen for the voice behind us. "Whether you turn to the right or to the left, your ears will hear a voice behind you, saying, 'This is the way; walk in it'" (Isaiah 30:21).

Rebellion is not reserved for headstrong prophets. No, all of us are subject to the perils of going our own way. As much as we'd like to believe otherwise, taking our own path can only lead to disorientation, confusion, and heartache. We find ourselves in shadow, in a blinding storm, or in a cloud bank. If we're not reoriented, we miss the path of God's purpose for us. Sometimes He allows us to be swallowed up by His mercy for our own protection. Remember, rebellion deserves death, so even if you are in an uncomfortable place due to your own choice, be thankful, like Jonah, for it may be the embodiment of God's mercy. Shift your gaze from your problem to your Provider. Allow His touch to reassure and guide you back to truth, back to His good purposes for your life.

If Jonah had not found his way again, would the Ninevites have been lost? All we know is that when Jonah did arrive, something about his presence and his message shocked the evil empire to its core. The shaken king decreed, "Do not let any man or beast, herd or flock, taste anything; do not let them eat or drink. But let man and beast be covered with sackcloth. Let everyone call urgently on God. Let them give up their evil ways and their violence. Who knows? God may yet relent and with compassion turn from his fierce anger so that we will not perish" (Jonah 3:7–9).

Scripture goes on to add how God responded to that change of heart. "When God saw what they did and how they turned from their evil ways, he had compassion and did not bring upon them the destruction he had threatened" (v. 10). For at least a generation to follow, Nineveh walked in God's mercy.

Because Jonah had become oriented by the touch of God, a mighty city found its way, at least for a short season, into repentance and great grace.

How lost in the darkness can you be before you're beyond help, beyond hope? What if you rebelled not once, as Jonah did, but lived in complete rebellion for all your days? That's a different matter, of course. Or is it? The following story assures us that God will go a long, long, long way to touch someone who is lost and can't find his way home.

Cry from the Dungeon

Manasseh was the son of godly King Hezekiah of Judah, inheriting the throne from his father. He was the thirteenth king of Judah and reigned longer than any other Hebrew king.

Unfortunately, his long reign wasn't the only thing that put Manasseh into the record books. He also bears the distinction of being Judah's most wicked king. As far as Judah was concerned, he was Hitler, Stalin, and Saddam Hussein all wrapped up in one vile package.

It's surprising that Manasseh was so evil, knowing how good and godly his father was. Surely Manasseh grew up in a home where the God of Israel was honored and revered. Surely when he came of age, he joined his father in offering sacrifices. Certainly Manasseh had heard the daily psalms read and even sang the song of Moses. When he assumed the throne at age twelve, he most likely co-reigned with his father for nearly a decade. The influence of the Lord upon Manasseh, as both a growing young man and a king being groomed, is undeniable.

Yet sadly, that influence seemed only to impact him negatively. For whatever reason, it drove him the other way. Instead of walking in the spiritual footprints of his father, Manasseh seemed to lurch headlong into the evil ways of his grandfather, Ahaz. King Manasseh was not committed to the God of Israel, but rather committed himself to idolatry. He erected altars to Baal; he set up an image of the goddess Asherah in the sacred temple (where he almost certainly had joined his father in worship as a boy). His idolatry and depravity went so far that the hardhearted king even sacrificed his own son to the Ammonite god called Molech.

Anyone in the nation who spoke against Manasseh's evil actions was killed. Many even believe that the callous king had the prophet Isaiah put to death. I guess it's pretty clear by now that Manasseh was a bad dude! Unlike Jonah, who received God's word yet struggled with a temporary lapse in obedience, Manasseh practiced all-out rejection of God. He utterly turned his back on his godly heritage, and his heart increasingly hardened as he adopted false gods and evil practices. The Bible puts in a nutshell what Manasseh did. "But the people did not listen. Manasseh led them astray, so that they did more evil than the nations the LORD had destroyed before the Israelites" (2 Kings 21:9).

Just as Jonah's rebellion led to disorientation, so did Manasseh's rejection of God. Eventually, however, the judgment of a righteous God caught up to him. (By the way, it always does.) The evil king was taken captive by the Assyrians: "The LORD brought against them the army commanders of the king of Assyria, who took Manasseh prisoner, put a hook in his nose, bound him with bronze shackles and took him to Babylon" (2 Chronicles 33:10–11).

This was the kind of body piercing that will never be in style. The once proud king of Judah, arms and legs shackled in bronze, was pulled along the highway to Nineveh by a hook in his nose. He'd made his own reservations and chosen his own accommodations by turning his back on the God who loved him. The son of Hezekiah was now a captive of a mighty military state and was utterly without hope.

You see, when we choose to reject God, we eventually end up like Manasseh—captive, bound, and chained by feelings of hopelessness. We find that the life choices we have made are not worth the price we have to pay. Our hard hearts have led us to a place of utter desperation.

So how do we become oriented again?

How do we find freedom from the bondage our rejection has created?

Look at 2 Chronicles 33:12–13. To me, it's one of the most amazing passages in all the Bible.

> In his distress he [Manasseh] sought the favor of the LORD his God and humbled himself greatly before the God of his fathers. And when he prayed to him, the LORD was moved by his entreaty and listened to his plea; so he brought him back to Jerusalem and to his kingdom.

Manasseh was far from home, deep in the bowels of some awful dungeon, possibly chained to the wall, robbed of all light and hope.

Almost...

At a moment that must have been close to utter despair, the captive king remembered something. Something from childhood, perhaps. Something from his long-ago innocence. Maybe it was a psalm. Maybe it was a prayer. Maybe it was a promise. Whatever it was, he turned his heart to the God of his father. And he exercised just enough humble faith to invite God's guiding touch into his life.

You and I must do the same. No matter where we are in life. No matter what we've done or failed to do. No matter what circumstances in which we find ourselves entwined and bound. When we find ourselves in the disorienting darkness of our own captivity, we must humbly call upon our God. He stands ready to respond. His ear is always tilted toward us in anticipation of our humble cry for help. It's true! And He is willing to come and touch us if we will simply remember Him.

If you harbor any doubt of that fact, look at what happened when Manasseh prayed. It is the very thing that happens when you and I pray. "And when he prayed to him, the LORD was moved by his entreaty and listened to his plea" (v. 13).

It's almost like God is craning His neck over the portals of heaven, waiting to hear us call Him. He listens for even the voice of the one who has rejected Him. He is moved to respond even to the one who has forgotten Him. What a long-suffering and merciful God! When Manasseh remembered God, he was then mercifully delivered by the hand of God. "So he brought him back to Jerusalem and to his kingdom. Then Manasseh knew that the LORD is God" (v. 13).

Don't reject truth in your life, for it is truth that sets you free. When we reject truth and embrace lies, those very lies will lead us into captivity. We reject the Lord at great cost. We tend to sacrifice what is most sacred and precious to us on the altar of self-gratification. When we forget God, we tend to invest in idols that are fleeting and temporary, yet so very, very demanding. It might be a career or materialism, it might be chasing fame or fantasies, but it will always lead to bondage.

Accept the truth that leads to real freedom.

Don't reject your God.

Humble yourself and seek His favor.

When you do, His hand will reach directly from heaven into your heart. He will guide you out of your bondage and restore you.

Why would God touch a heathen king who wasn't worthy of mercy? The same reason He touches me and touches you. It's just what He does. It is the loving nature of God that compels Him to seek and save that which is lost. He doesn't lean back on His throne, watching and waiting to see how well we maneuver toward Him. No, we know that God's own Son left His throne, choosing to place Himself on a cross instead, just so we could feel His touch. He extends His hand of guidance, mercy, and bountiful forgiveness to all who simply glance toward heaven and acknowledge Him. Instead of rejecting Him, receive Him. Instead of elevating yourself and your accomplishments, elevate Him and watch Him accomplish "great and mighty things, which you do not know" (Jeremiah 33:3, NKJV).

Rebellion, rejection, and pride will land you in darkness. By faith, lift your hand to heaven and you will feel His touch. His hand will receive you, restore you, and guide you down the path of His purpose for you.

That "amen" you just heard from the grandstands was from Jonah and Manasseh…who learned these wonderful truths the hard way.

FIVE

His Redeeming Touch

"I need to hurry home. Today is *Gotcha Day!*"

Cinda, one of my new friends from the women's conference in Kentucky, made that excited announcement as we were wheeling our luggage out the door.

Gotcha Day? I mused. *What in the world is Gotcha Day?*

I raced through my mental calendar—and no such holiday emerged from memory. But maybe I hadn't heard her right. Maybe she was a completed Jew and had actually said it's *Matzo* Day. Or perhaps Gotcha Day was actually German (or Norwegian or Polish) for Saturday…or something.

Finally I couldn't stand it any longer. "All right, you knew I was going to ask! Now what in the world is 'Gotcha Day'?"

Cinda giggled. She reminded me that her two precious children were adopted. Gotcha Day is a huge and joyful celebration commemorating the day the children joined the family. In their household, Gotcha Day is just as big as a birthday. Maybe bigger. What a marvelous reason to have a party!

My Gotcha Day was March 25, 1973.

I know specifically when it was, because I chose to be "gotten." No, I wasn't adopted into my earthly family (my mom has hospital bills to prove otherwise!). I was adopted into the family of God when I was only nine years old. I remember vividly the place of my invitation—and even wrote down the time it occurred on the single page separating the Old and New Testaments in my first Bible.

It was 8:35 P.M.

That's the very moment I felt God's redeeming touch upon me as He gently pulled me close to His heart and made me His very own. It is as real to me today as it was in those long-ago days of childhood.

That was the moment and the day I could say, "Abba, Father."

Father Without the Filter

Sometimes we base our perception of who Father God is upon our earthly father. If you grew up with a dad who was harsh or distant, you might attribute those same qualities to your heavenly Father. If your earthly dad was absent as you grew up—or indifferent or passive or cold—it might be hard to believe that God is ever-present, constantly loving and caring for you.

If, on the other hand, you grew up with a dad who was kind, loving, and consistent, it may be a little easier to step into a trusting relationship with your unseen heavenly Father. But let me assure you, regardless of the kind of earthly dad you have or had, God is a good and loving Father who will always be there for you.

A little girl named Kirsten taught me a lesson about God's love—and His redeeming touch. Just a few days shy of Kirsten's second birthday, her mother, Debbi, was taken to heaven because of pregnancy complications. Such a devastating loss shakes each of us in the deepest part of our understanding. I'm sure Kirsten's father, Scott, walked a difficult path carved out by tears and tenacity.

People from the church rallied around Scott. Lots of

women offered to help care for Kirsten. One of those women was Marcey.

Marcey was in her late twenties and single. She was vivacious, bright, and generous. During the year that followed Debbi's death, Scott and Marcey forged a friendship. Their friendship became affection; their affection, love.

On August 26, 2000, Scott kissed Marcey for the first time as they stood together at the altar as bride and groom.

Not long after this, Marcey and three-year-old Kirsten were traveling in the car together. "Mommy?" Kirsten said. "I used to call you Marcey and now I call you Mommy. Why?"

Marcey's mind raced with all the possible answers explaining Debbi's death. She finally summed it up by saying, "Because I love you."

That's what it truly means to be a daughter. We are loved. You and I were once distant from God; our sin alienated us from relationship with Him. We knew of Him as Creator and Judge—great and high and fearsome—but now through Jesus we know Him as Father.

Why?

Because He loves us.

It's not because of our striving or our merit that we are seated in heavenly places with Him. It's just because He loves us.

Little Kirsten didn't have to earn Marcey's love. On August 26, when Marcey said "I do" to Scott, she also said an "I do" to Kirsten, simply out of love. On the day you entered God's family, the Father said an unconditional "I do" to you, and the steadfast love of our Lord never changes.

Even though God's love never changes, sometimes our lives do. Relationships change, circumstances spin out of our control, and we find ourselves feeling alone. Maybe you have experienced lonely times in recent days. Perhaps you've found yourself alone in the car or doing some tedious task at home or even on a busy sidewalk, and you felt that little ache in some empty place in your heart and wondered if God was really there and if He really took notice of you. Oh my friend, He was there. In that moment. Your Father was there in His fullness as surely as He is on His throne in heaven, surrounded by mighty angels. You may have felt alone, but you were not!

> Because God has said, "Never will I leave you; never will I forsake you." So we say with confidence, "The Lord is my helper; I will not be afraid."
>
> Hebrews 13:5–6

He is not insensitive, but is kind and caring. He is a promise maker and a promise keeper. Praise be to your good Father who loves you with an everlasting love.

In the days of my physical sight, I can remember looking at someone I knew very well and suddenly seeing him or her in a whole new way. Some aspect of physical appearance or personality seemed to suddenly shine forth, and it was as though I was seeing that person with fresh eyes.

How long has it been since you've seen God with fresh eyes? There is so much to see, so much to know, so much to experience, so many aspects to His character, so many facets to His love.

Have you looked at Him lately? Have you really seen Him for who He is, rather than viewing Him through the filters of others—or even that of your own earthly father? John tells us that "God is love." Think about a few qualities of that love as you read 1 Corinthians 13. Think about it as a portrait of your heavenly Father.

Your Father is patient and kind.
He does not envy or boast.
Your Father is not proud or rude.
He is not self-seeking.
Your Father is not easily angered.
Your Father keeps no record of wrongs.
He does not delight in evil.
He rejoices with the truth.

Your Father always protects, always trusts, always hopes, always perseveres.

Your Father never fails.

Just because He loves you, He calls you His own. He is a good Father, completely trustworthy and loving. He longs to lavish you with all the benefits of His glorious inheritance.

He has touched your life, and that touch was a redeeming touch…drawing you out of darkness…breaking the chains of habit and self-defeating behavior…offering you life instead of death, security instead of fear and despair. Can you sense His hand on yours right now, warm and strong?

You are a child, chosen and dearly loved. Thank your God for the privilege of calling Him "Father."

> To show that you are his sons, God sent the Spirit of his Son into our hearts, the Spirit who cries out, "Father, my Father."
>
> Galatians 4:6, TEV

Because He Said So

I understood God's redeeming touch more clearly after spending a week in Black Mountain, North Carolina, with my friends Mark and Katharyn Richt. You see, Mark and Katharyn are the proud parents of three sons and one daughter, who was adopted.

Anya joined the Richt household when she was three years old. She was born with a severe facial deformity that causes the left side of her sweet face to protrude and sag unnaturally. Her breathing is labored since part of her nose is collapsed. Her mouth is misshapen and difficult to use.

As Anya has gotten older, she has come to understand that her face looks different from other children's. She undoubtedly overhears the whispers, snickers, and cruel words. But Anya has a fortitude that carries her forward into her future despite second glances and glaring stares.

Prompted by Katharyn, I asked this dear little girl, "Anya, what do you look like?"

"I'm beautiful," she answered. Then she paused and said, "Because my papa says I am."

You see, every day, Anya's big old football coach daddy tells her that she is beautiful, and Anya simply believes it. It doesn't matter what anyone else thinks or says, her papa says she's beautiful...and he only tells the truth.

That's what your Father says about you, too. He loves you and calls you His own. And He thinks you're beautiful. He chose you just the way you were, rescued you from an orphan's future, and gave you His own name. *Choose to see Him as He is. For He sees you as the treasured child He has chosen.*

Psalm 45:11 says, "The king is enthralled by your beauty." We're beautiful to God because He loves us. Just think, not many can claim that their father is a king, but you can! Honor Him by believing that He is who He says He is. Honor Him by embracing Him as the good and loving Father He wants to be in your life, for He chose you to be His own.

"BROUGHT NEAR"

I remember one of my earliest conversations with my friend Christin as we watched our children play. She told me that all she ever wanted in life was to be a wife and a mother. She and Lane, her husband, had dreamed and planned that they would have a household full of kids since their engagement!

Three months before their wedding, however, doctors discovered tumors extending from her diaphragm to her bladder. Amidst bridal showers and wedding plans, Christin had major surgery, which included the removal of an ovary. For the first seven years of their marriage, she was plagued by many more tumors—and five additional surgeries, which included a complete hysterectomy at the age of twenty-eight.

Christin had to mourn the devastating loss of her dream to be pregnant. Now, instead of wearing maternity clothes, she and Lane would don traveling clothes!

They discovered that over six hundred thousand children in Russian orphanages needed a mommy and a daddy. They began the adoption process and were led to a little boy in a Russian orphanage. In June 1999, they received a video of a tiny baby boy lying on his tummy looking at the camera with eyes as big as quarters.

"From the very first sight of that little boy," Christin said, "we knew he was ours. Nothing is harder than knowing your child is somewhere in the world alive, but you aren't with him."

Six weeks later, that family of two boarded an airplane and began the long journey to Russia—where they would become a family of three. As they entered the orphanage, they were handed their precious son.

"Lane and I could barely see him," Christin recounted, "because our eyes were full of tears! We were finally parents!" Little Joshua was tiny and malnourished. At six months old, he weighed only eight and a half pounds.

I have a feeling that the sentiments of Christin's heart reflect the sentiments of God's heart. He knew us and longed for us even when we were far away. His heart must ache knowing that His son or His daughter is in the world alive but not with Him.

Paul wrote:

> Remember that at that time you were separate from Christ...without hope and without God in the world. But now in Christ Jesus you who once were far away have been *brought near* through the blood of Christ.
>
> Ephesians 2:12–13

Brought near! That's what a redeeming touch is all about! It reaches across an impossible chasm, grasps something lost and far away, and brings it home as a treasure. God, who desires to be our Father, went to unimaginable lengths to draw us to Himself. He laid His own Son upon a cross to bridge that great chasm separating us from Him. He came to us when we were abandoned, orphaned, and alone. He found us, small and needy, and made us His own. He embraced us and held us in His heart. "Long ago, even before he made the world, God loved us and chose us in Christ.... His unchanging plan has always been to adopt us into his own family by bringing us to himself through Jesus Christ" (Ephesians 1:4–5, NLT).

We are all like Joshua, waiting to be "gotten"! We matter to our Father God, who rescues us just as we are. As an energetic three-and-a-half-year-old, Joshua frequently tells his baby story:

Once upon a time, there was a mommy and daddy who wanted a baby so bad, so they prayed that Jesus would give them a baby. God sent them a picture and they got on a plane and flew all the way to Brussia and got their baby and held on tight. They flew all the way back and had a big party at the airport.

Our story is like his. Our Father loved us so much that He came and got us, and heaven threw a big party on our Gotcha Day! Jesus told a similar story to the tax collectors, sinners, and Pharisees who had gathered to hear Him as He traveled through Capernaum. Jesus asked them,

> "Suppose one of you has a hundred sheep and loses one of them. Does he not leave the ninety-nine in the open country and go after the lost sheep until he finds it? And when he finds it, he joyfully puts it on his shoulders and goes home. Then he calls his friends and neighbors together and says, 'Rejoice with me; I have found my lost sheep.' I tell you that in the same way there will be more rejoicing in heaven over one sinner who repents than over ninety-nine righteous persons who do not need to repent."
>
> LUKE 15:4–7

You are that one lost sheep. You are so valuable to the Good Shepherd that He pursues you, scoops you up into His arms, and rejoices. You may not feel worthy of a party in your honor, but that's exactly what happens! For millennia the halls of heaven have resonated with the sound of great rejoicing each time an orphan comes home.

Don't ever underestimate whose rejoicing in heaven is the loudest. I'm sure the angels blow their trumpets and exclaim "Hallelujah!" I can almost hear the saints that have gone before clapping, cheering, and praising. But I think one voice is heard above the gleeful exaltation. A voice like joyful thunder. It must be the voice of Father God leading the welcome home chorus. He loves you. Thanks be to God for His unspeakable gift.

Little Joshua began to pray and ask for a baby sister, so in February 2002 a baby from Guatemala became the latest addition to the Harrison household. For four long months before the adoption, Christin would receive photos of her little Bethany. With every letter and picture, Christin's heart ached and she longed for her baby girl. On February 12, her longing was fulfilled as she cradled baby Bethany for the first time. God crafted and grafted together a beautiful family born from His loving heart. Joshua is now a proud and protective big brother, and Bethany is a busy toddler.

So as I visit with Christin on the sofa, surrounded by toys, sippy cups, and lots of noise, I hear something special in her voice as she tells her story. I hear gratefulness and love. She uniquely understands what it means to be "chosen." And her children will also understand someday how incredibly blessed they have been to be chosen by parents who love them.

Because of our adoption, we too must celebrate that we are chosen.

CHOSEN AND SEALED

Prone to foolish pride as we are, we might think of ourselves as something special because we have forsaken everything and chosen Christ. But consider the words of Jesus as recorded by the apostle John. "You did not choose me, but I chose you" (John 15:16). These words ought to shatter our foolish vanities forever—and provoke us to pure wonder. You might think it wonderful that a man or woman should choose God. But the reality is far more stunning. The wonder is that God should choose us.

Adoption is the perfect picture of what it means to be chosen. In the days of ancient of Rome, when the New Testament was penned, the adoption process was elaborate and intensive; when it was completed, the adoption was absolute. The person who had been adopted enjoyed all the privileges of a legitimate son in his new family. His rights and responsibilities from his old family were completely relinquished. It was as if he were a new person. He carried no old debts or former obligations.

And that's what God did for us! "Therefore, if anyone is in Christ, he is a new creation; the old has gone, the new has come!" (2 Corinthians 5:17). We once were under the authority of sin and despair, but since our adoption we now thrive under the shade and protection of our new family tree! That means we belong to God. "Now it is God who makes both us and you stand firm in Christ. He anointed us, set his seal of ownership on us, and put his Spirit in our hearts as a deposit, guaranteeing what is to come" (1:21–22). That means God not only chose you to be part of His family; He went a step further and placed His seal of ownership on you.

A seal was an emblem used to show ownership in ancient culture. Men of authority wore a signet ring or medallion that bore their personal mark. Their seal indicated security and permanency. Documents were not viewed as authentic until they were marked with a seal. Seals made of wax, moist clay, or ink were used to authenticate covenants, contracts, decrees, and other legal documents. The ancient seal was used just like our signature is used today: It identified the owner, represented a promise, and guaranteed authenticity.

On the day of our adoption, we too were sealed.

Can you feel the warm wax? Can you sense the gentle pressure of God's signet ring...sealing you as His own for all of time and eternity?

God placed His seal upon us. He signed His name upon our hearts and marked us as His own. Paul put it this way when he wrote to the Ephesians: "And you also were included in Christ when you heard the word of truth, the gospel of your salvation. Having believed, you were marked in him with a seal, the promised Holy Spirit" (1:13).

You weren't the only one chosen—consider those who bore God's seal of ownership through the ages. Remember Abraham. Remember Peter. Those were their *new* names, the names God gave them because He had chosen them. Abraham was originally Abram (Genesis 17:5). Peter was first named Simon (John 1:42). And there are others. God called Jacob by the name Israel. And even the apostle Paul was first known as Saul.

Because you are chosen, you also have a new name. Daniel put it this way when he prayed, "Your people bear your Name" (Daniel 9:19). You bear God's name. You are sealed by Him. You have been chosen.

My friend Christin marveled at that very thought. "I think about what our lives would have been like if God had not chosen to take the details of Joshua and Bethany's lives and the details of ours and bring them all together." We should all marvel at what God has done for each of us—merging the details of our lives with His detailed plan. The result is an inheritance of love. Have you grasped how grand your adoption is?

You are now a forever child of the heavenly Father, and "neither death nor life, neither angels nor demons, neither the present nor the future, nor any powers, neither height nor depth, nor anything else in all creation, will be able to separate us from the love of God that is in Christ Jesus" (Romans 8:38–39). You are now joint heirs with Jesus. "You are no longer foreigners and aliens, but fellow citizens with God's people and members of God's household" (Ephesians 2:19). May we never cease to wonder at such an inheritance.

Since the first time I felt His redeeming touch, I have been deeply in love with my Father and with every word He speaks. I still marvel at this and am still captivated by the truth and compassion of His Word. I weep often in church as we sing the lyrics "Thank You for the cross, my Friend." For it was that very cross, and the willingness of Jesus, that made my adoption possible.

I walked straight into the throne room of my new Father through the costly doorway of the rugged cross. Now, every time I think about how I was "gotten," a sense of humble celebration wells up in my heart.

For the past thirty years, I have remembered each March 25. I quietly celebrate that "I am my beloved's, and my beloved is mine" (Song of Solomon 6:3, NKJV).

But I think from now on I will celebrate a little louder—and maybe you should, too. After all, "Gotcha Day" changed our lives! We passed from death to life, traded our sorrow for His joy, received hope that transcends reason, and glimpsed grace that is truly amazing. Because we too were "gotten," we will also one day excitedly announce, "I need to hurry home."

For the ultimate celebration is when we finally walk up those last steps of our Father's front porch, step through the open door, and enter His house forever.

SIX

Shaped by His Hand

My assistant's voice trailed off as she finished reading the final words of the article.

It was a magazine piece about me, and this was our first chance to read the results of the writer's extensive interviews.

The flatness in Katie's voice mirrored my own disappointment.

"Do you like it?" she asked.

"It's okay."

It was quiet for a minute or so before I suddenly blurted out my real feelings.

"Katie, I *don't* like it! I don't like it at all!"

"Me neither!" she followed. "It's about your blindness…it's not about *you*. And—there's a difference."

Katie was right on target. Many articles have been written about my journey into darkness, but this one seemed to exploit the enigma of sight loss. It almost seemed to paint me as part of some circus sideshow—mixing me in with the world's shortest man and the "incredible two-headed woman."

I'll be honest: I don't like to be defined by my blindness.

To me, it's just another facet of who I am. I'm a woman. I'm a wife. I'm a mother. I'm a singer and songwriter. I'm an author. I'm a highlighted brunette (thanks to L'Oréal convincing me that I'm worth it!). I'm five foot three (almost). I'm trying to be more like Jesus.

And yes…I'm blind.

The article was published and, thankfully, has slipped into obscurity. But I will always remember it because it exposed something deep within me.

I resented being characterized by my blindness. I suppose I still do.

I embrace my blindness because it *refines* me. It is God who has permitted this hardship in my life, and it is

God who uses it every day to shape, mold, and train me. The process isn't always pleasant, but the prize is worth it. I believe that God moved upon my life with the finesse of an artist and the practiced hand of a sculptor. He allowed me to bear this affliction from age fifteen, not so I would be defined by it but so I could become refined through it. The blindness is not meant to characterize me, but to produce character in me.

The writer of Hebrews put it this way: *"Endure hardship as discipline;* God is treating you as sons" (12:7, emphasis mine). Did you catch that? This is what the Bible says about facing hardship. All hardship. Any hardship. Including family troubles. Including financial heartaches. Including health struggles. Including blindness. Including whatever it is you might be facing today.

You see, God can and will use hardship to discipline us. When you hear the word *discipline,* however, don't automatically think of punishment. To assume that hardship in our lives is a punishment rendered by the harsh hand of God is to misunderstand His character. No, discipline is the same as training. In fact, the Greek word translated *discipline* in this verse is also translated as *nurture* (Ephesians 6:4) and *instruction* (2 Timothy 3:16). God works through the difficult situations in our lives to teach, shape, and mold us.

And so He will…if we let Him.

The Bible says that we are like clay and God is the potter. He uses the pressure of trials and heartache—the measured, careful pressure from His hands—to create a beautiful vessel.

FOUR RESPONSES

God often uses affliction, painful though it may be, to perfect us. The writer of Hebrews knew this very well as he penned His letter to these Jewish believers. He knew they were under great strain and persecution.

> Remember those earlier days after you had received the light, when you stood your ground in a great contest in the face of suffering. Sometimes you were publicly exposed to insult and persecution; at other times you stood side by side with those who were so treated. You sympathized with those in prison and joyfully accepted the confiscation of your property, because you knew that you yourselves had better and lasting possessions.
>
> HEBREWS 10:32–34

He also knew that we all grow weary in the midst of hardship. Our heads begin to droop and our knees begin to wobble. We begin looking over our shoulder and think about turning back. So he encouraged these discouraged saints to continue to respond with faithfulness in their adversity. Listen to his words: "No discipline seems pleasant at the time, but painful. Later on, however, it produces a harvest of righteousness and peace for those who have been trained by it" (12:11).

None of us enjoy pain and trials. In fact, most of us are grieved by them. They push and pull us. They bend us out of shape. But even so, we should never forget that they have vast potential to bring benefit to our lives, depending on our response to the discipline.

According to Hebrews 12, pressure and trials will force us into one of four different identities.

1. The flippant fatalist

This is an individual who disregards hardship, simply passing it off as the law of averages. "Everybody has trouble. Stuff happens. It's just my lot in life." Half a century ago, Doris Day hit the charts singing, "Que sera, sera / Whatever will be, will be." In today's jargon, we'd just roll our eyes and say, "Whatever." Instead of receiving the message God seeks to convey within the suffering, the fatalist simply passes it off with a sigh and a shrug.

The writer of Hebrews, however, warns us not to do that!

He specifically tells us, "Do not make light of the Lord's discipline" (12:5). In other words, don't lightly regard what He is doing in your life through trials and pressing circumstances. Instead of assuming that our suffering is just a meaningless part of life, random and capricious, instead of just saying, "Well, I guess it's my turn," *we should seek to redeem our heartache.* We should ask God to enlighten our eyes so we can read between the lines! When we do, we begin to discern the message and learn the lesson of our affliction.[1] Instead of being flippant, we are to be fortified by His strong hand—like Job. "Blessed is the man whom God corrects; so do not despise the discipline of the Almighty.... But he knows the way that I take; when he has tested me, I will come forth as gold" (Job 5:17; 23:10).

2. The frail fainter

Lots of us become fainters when the fire of trials gets hot. We simply collapse and quit! We pick up our marbles and go home. I've heard this called the "crybaby reaction." If you listen closely, you can hear the frail fainter lamenting

---

1.The apostle James, speaking to those who were enduring "trials of many kinds" (James 1:2), urged these suffering believers to seek God's wisdom and perspective in the midst of their circumstances. Constantly asking "Why me?" is not a helpful prayer. But Scripture does not discourage us from praying, "What's going on, Lord? What's this all about? What do You want me to learn?"

out loud: "*Why* did *this* happen to *me?* WHY? I can't take it anymore.... It's just not worth living the Christian life if this is how it is." You get the picture; the frail fainter simply fades and eventually faints. But the Bible tells us, "Do *not* lose heart when he rebukes you" (Hebrews 12:5).

You and I need not whine or wither when we feel the pressure build or the temperature rise. No, let me remind you of who you are according to God's Word: "But we are not of those who shrink back and are destroyed, but of those who believe and are saved" (10:39). Instead of fainting, have faith. Cling (with your fingernails and toenails and all that you are) to the good and faithful hand of your God. Scramble up on that Rock that is higher than you—higher than anything or anybody! (See Psalm 61:2.) Set your hope on the fact that He will sustain you and strengthen you, no matter what you are facing, no matter what life delivers to your front door.

We've all had occasion in our life scripts to read the part of the fatalist or the fainter. I know I have! Thankfully, though, none of us has been typecast! Children of the King are neither destined nor designed to shrivel up and die in the midst of their heartache. There are actually two more responses we can and should choose according to Hebrews 12.

3. The faithful follower

The third response is *faithfulness.* As we already noted, the writer of Hebrews tells us to "endure hardship as discipline; God is treating you as sons" (12:7). Sometimes we see the word *endure,* and it conjures up pictures of a Christian couch potato—nursing her wounds and barely hanging on. But that's not what this word means.

This isn't a passive, laid-back word at all! In its original language, *endure* actually means "to actively persevere." It's the same word Paul uses in Romans 2:7, which is translated as "patient continuance" (KJV). James 1:2–3 tells us that it is a result of the testing of our faith: "Consider it pure joy, my brothers, whenever you face trials of many kinds, because you know that the testing of your faith develops perseverance." You see, it is a proactive, keep marching, don't-give-up kind of word! It's the very picture of faithfulness.

Oh, my dear friend, don't shrug off your trials or chalk them up to random bad luck.

Don't quit. Don't throw in the towel. Don't faint.

Keep your shoes on and walk with perseverance. Remain faithful, for there is a reward beyond imagination waiting for you if you do. "Blessed is the man who perseveres under trial, because when he has stood the test, he will receive the crown of life that God has promised to those who love him" (James 1:12).

4. The fruitful finisher

The last response to the discipline of hardship is found in Hebrews 12:11. It is *fruitfulness.* "Later on, however, it [hardship, trials, struggles] produces a harvest of righteousness and peace for those who have been trained by it." For all of us who don't faint and miss the message written in our heartache, we will become fruitful as we remain faithful. Our fruitfulness, however, is dependent upon whether or not we choose to be trained by our heartache.

Note that the harvest of righteousness and peace is not an automatic result of enduring the crush of great difficulty. No, only those who have chosen to be "trained" (molded or refined) by their affliction are the ones who experience a great reward. Please hear me: *When we choose to remain on the Potter's wheel and rest within the Potter's hands, we begin to reflect the Potter's handiwork.*

> These have come so that your faith—of greater worth than gold, which perishes even though refined by fire—may be proved genuine and may result in praise, glory and honor when Jesus Christ is revealed.
>
> 1 PETER 1:7

How foolish it would be for us to become stiff and hardened beneath the gentle pressure of the Potter's hands. To complain and rebel against the refining touch of God only disposes us to greater discontent. The fruit of righteousness is sweet and satisfying. Don't miss the opportunity to taste it! It will bring nourishment and refreshment to you as you persevere. Allow your difficulties and trials to train you and discipline you. For when you do, you will see the glory of God displayed.

Canvas for His Glory

We should never assume that uncommon calamities are some kind of punishment for sin. In fact, they are a canvas upon which God can illustrate the many shades of His grace and glory.

In John 9, the disciples ask Jesus a penetrating question when they encounter a man blind since birth. "Rabbi, who sinned, this man or his parents, that he was born blind?" (v. 2). Our Lord's answer to His disciples are the very words I often hear whispered in my ear. "'Neither this man nor his parents sinned,' said Jesus, 'but this happened so that the work of God might be displayed in his life'" (v. 3).

When hardship refines you, God's glory shines forth—like a sudden shaft of sunlight through a heavy curtain of clouds. People marveled at the miracle of this man's restored sight. The healed man himself fumbled for an explanation as the Pharisees confronted him. All he could say was, "One thing I do know. I was blind but now I see!" (v. 25).

I'm convinced that the work of God can be displayed in my blindness, too—even if God chooses not to show His glory through healing me. Yes, it's an undeniable miracle for blind eyes to see. But God also shows Himself strong in the life of someone who suffers—through no fault of her own—and still remains faithful. It captivates us to see someone confined and constrained by trials and calamity and still bear the fruit of peace and righteousness. That's when God's glory is truly seen, because it can only be God fashioning such beauty from the elements of certain despair.

God is wise in allowing calamity and heartache. It becomes His refining touch upon our lives. The touch of a Potter's hands.

The Artisan's Touch

Over and over in Scripture, you and I are referred to as dust or clay. It's easy to understand why. If you go back to the beginning, you realize that "the LORD God formed the man from the dust of the ground and breathed into his nostrils the breath of life, and the man became a living being" (Genesis 2:7). In Psalms, we're reminded that God "remembers that we are dust" (103:14). Paul even refers to us as earthen vessels or "jars of clay" (2 Corinthians 4:7). In its most rudimentary form, clay isn't that impressive, but when molded by a potter, artfully shaped, and refined by fire, you have a work of art.

We know that what makes an earthen vessel lovely is the consistent and purposeful pressure of the potter's hand. But just as we saw in Hebrews, that process can be painful. Imagine a shapeless lump of clay. It's placed on the potter's wheel as a roundish lump—hardly more than an indistinct blob. And then the potter goes to work—pushing, pulling, molding, centering the clay on the wheel. As that process continues, the clay is transformed from its unformed, natural state…and formed into something lovely and useful.

That's what God does for us. He takes us into His loving hands and crafts us into something supernatural. That's why we experience such pain sometimes. Yes, let's be real here: *The refining touch of God in our lives may not only be highly uncomfortable; it may also hurt—and hurt deeply.* It might require us to bend in ways we never anticipated. It might compel us to yield and stretch to the very breaking point.

Maybe you've been there recently. Maybe you're there right now. You're wondering how the pain you've been enduring can possibly produce anything other than ruin and ashes in your life. I understand. I've been there, too!

I'll never forget a certain date with Phil, back when we were in college. We'd been dating a little more than a year when one fateful evening he invited me out to dinner. As we sat in the front seat of his old '66 Dodge, he began to tell me something—something I could immediately sense was hard for him to say.

I remember asking myself, *What's happening here? Is he going to break up with me? Or is he going to propose?* It was neither of those. Instead, he said something that caught me totally by surprise.

"Jennifer, I've noticed something that—I need to discuss with you. You are awfully negative." As he continued to explain what he had observed, my mind was reeling! *How dare he?!*

After all, I thought I was in pretty good shape. I wasn't a pessimist. I was a *realist.* Everyone in their right mind knew the glass was most certainly half empty! Only dewy-eyed Pollyannas went around seeing the glass half full. At that moment, however, my "half-empty glass" was starting to boil. I was furious! I tried to listen to his reason as he gently explained my deficiencies. He even gave examples! I argued, justified, and tried to shift the conversation to his faults. What I really wanted to do was dump my half-empty glass of water onto his sanctimonious head.

As you can imagine, that date didn't end very well. An Arctic cold front gripped the interior of Philip's Dodge, and we soon called it a night.

We temporarily patched things up the next day and moved on. But I'll be honest with you: That conversation haunted me for years. Eventually, many miles down life's road, it finally prodded me to see my own reflection in the half-empty glass. As painful and embarrassing as that front-seat confrontation was, it brought forth something pleasant and fruitful in my life. God used the painful truth of Phil's words to turn my natural pessimism into supernatural optimism.

It's okay to be rebuked and corrected by our Father. It's a sign that He regards us as His very own. Sometimes God allows hard things to come into our lives to refine us, and sometimes He allows us to receive hard truths so He can correct us and form us into a vessel that radiates His glory.

THE TOUCH OF MERCY

The refining touch of God's hand doesn't always mean pressure and pain. Sometimes He overwhelms us (and brings us to our knees) with the touch of His mercy.

This is the touch that not only refines us, but also falls softly on our spirits and fills our hearts with awe.

In a small Georgia town in late 1969, I felt such a touch. Amidst friends and family in the backyard of our Manchester home, I sat in the sandbox with Jerry. Like six-year-olds do, Jerry and I had shaped castles with our tiny hands and boundless imaginations. All was well on that warm southern afternoon as my folks sipped sweet tea with the neighbors while Jerry and I played.

Until something clicked in Jerry's young mind and he made a fatal move.

Yes, his testosterone had lain dormant for too long, because suddenly—with one fluid and unexpected motion—he decapitated my castle with his little blue shovel.

I was stunned. Wrath flooded my little heart. I began to correct his Neanderthal behavior at the top of my lungs. His response? Instead of throwing some choice words back in my direction, he threw a handful of gritty, warm sand.

I figure it was about this time that our unsuspecting parents tuned in. I wish their timing had been delayed, but I'm sure they caught a 20/20 view of my throwing a handful of sand back at Jerry.

But wouldn't you know it? My handful of sand—unintentionally, I assure you—went right into Jerry's eyes! He began to scream, parents began to run, and my impending doom drew near. All would have been fine if my dad had not asked the question that followed. After all, it was obvious that Jerry, the Neanderthal, had started this fiasco. I was simply defending my honor.

"Jennifer, did you throw sand in Jerry's eyes?"

"NO!"

"Jenna, I *saw* you. Now I'm asking you again. Did you throw sand in Jerry's eyes?"

A tearful but unwavering "No!" was my reply.

Dad then proceeded to explain how lying was far worse than even throwing sand. He prodded and coached, but I would not concede. So as Jerry's eyes were being flushed with water from the garden hose, my dad told me to head inside for my punishment.

He interrupted my tearful march up to the porch. "Before you go in, you need to pick a switch." For those of you who aren't aware of what a switch is...lucky you! A switch is a tender branch from a tree. To make it effective, you have to strip the leaves from it. Then it's used for spanking! Now, I know the world has changed in the past few decades, and corporal punishment is a bit out of vogue. But in Georgia in the late sixties, the switch was still very much in vogue. Before you panic and assume that this was abuse, let me tell you that the switch was seldom used.

The switch's real power of persuasion was not in its sweeping across your backside. It was in the dread-filled act of actually picking one off the tree and presenting it to Dad. I pulled a tender branch from a dogwood tree and marched solemnly up the wooden staircase. I sat on my bed, switch in hand, waiting for my father to ascend those stairs. *This was going to hurt!*

In a few moments my dad arrived and sat next to me on the bed. He talked to me about how serious lying was—and even told me he thought Jerry deserved the sand I threw!

I finally admitted I had lied and told Dad I was sorry.

He asked me to hand him the switch.

I did. I knew I deserved a spanking because I had lied. But I will never forget what my father did next. He held the switch between his two hands and with the flair and grace of a martial artist, he *broke* it. Right before my wondering eyes, the punishment I had dreaded was no more.

He then began to explain mercy to me.

He told me that when Jesus died on the cross, He received what we deserved so we could receive something we didn't deserve. You see, Jesus didn't deserve death; He was sinless. You and I don't deserve pardon, for we are sinful.

When my sweet southern daddy held that broken branch before me, he illustrated mercy. I have never forgotten the tender touch of my father on that day. I know what mercy looks like. I saw it. I know what mercy sounds like, because I heard the snap of the broken branch. I know what mercy feels like, because it drew me close to the father who could have punished me.

To this day, the merciful touch of my heavenly Father draws me to Him. "He does not treat us as our sins deserve or repay us according to our iniquities" (Psalm 103:10).

Through the years of my life, I have been through fire and I have been through darkness, and with these tools He has refined me. But I have also been to the cross and experienced mercy beyond logic, beyond calculation.

And with this He broke my heart.

SEVEN

Stay Under the Touch

Through the centuries our Father's touch has been tender and steadfast, intentional and kind. Since the time He used His hands to form us out of dust, God has continued to reach down to man. He shelters us in His arms and offers Himself to us as the ultimate city of refuge. Superb craftsman that He is, He continually molds, shapes, and refines us. Every one of us is a "work in progress"—and will be until that best-of-all-days when we step through heaven's gate.

His touch has lifted, comforted, and sustained me through some of the most anxious and lonely moments of my life. And now that I know what God's embrace feels like, I will tell you this: *I never want to settle for less.*

We love His touch. We don't want the warmth of that touch to fade. How, then, can we make sure it doesn't? If you're looking for a complex theological answer to that question, you won't get one from me. The way I read it in the Bible, the solution is really pretty simple: *Stay as close to Him as you can.*

I think Moses said it as well as anyone: "Love the LORD your God, listen to his voice, and hold fast to him. For the LORD is your life" (Deuteronomy 30:20).

That's how we remain in the warmth of His touch. We must hold fast to Him, for He is our life. To "hold fast" literally means to cleave, cling, and stay close to God. In contemporary terminology, it means to hang with Him. Just like a little child wraps herself around her daddy's legs, we too are to wrap our hopes, our desires, our plans, and the very fabric of our lives around Him.

David knew all about holding fast. Alone in a desolate wilderness, he wrote: "My soul clings to you; your right hand upholds me" (Psalm 63:8). One contemporary paraphrase puts the verse like this: "I hold on to you for dear life" *(The Message).*

Jesus invited His followers to cling to Him also when

He said, "Remain in me, and I will remain in you" (John 15:4). If you listen closely, you can hear Him extending the same invitation to you. He longs for us to remain in Him; He wants us to abide with Him. That's why He touches us. It's not out of condescending benevolence. No, He touches us to draw us near.

I'm reminded of that oft-quoted verse from the book of Revelation, when our Lord says, "Behold, I stand at the door and knock; if anyone hears My voice and opens the door, I will come in to him and will dine with him, and he with Me" (3:20, NASB).

He knocks. Of course He does. None of us draw near to our God apart from His initiative, His wooing, His touch, His calling. He truly desires our fellowship. He wants us to invite Him into our lives for extended times of walking, talking, and sharing. The word for *dine* in this passage speaks of the principal meal of the day—a leisurely supper on an unhurried evening, not a quick burger at the drive-through.

Learning to abide has been a lesson that has stretched through the years for me—and sometimes I wonder if I've graduated from first grade. Oddly enough, a cat named Snowy helped me along the path to understanding.

Many years ago, we were given a preowned, prenamed tabby cat. He was a hefty male with a Garfield-like attitude.

But when we first brought him home he was scared. He smushed his oversized kitty body under the two-inch opening beneath the china cabinet. All the treats and catnip in Wal-Mart could not coerce him to come out. He meowed day and night, and we felt so sorry for him, displaced and disoriented as he was. Then one morning when we got up, he wasn't there. Instead, we heard a slightly more confident meow coming from somewhere else in the house. Under my bed!

Snowy had decided to make the best of it—and adopt me. I was his new companion. Where I walked, he walked. When I stopped, he stopped. If I sat for a spell, within seconds his fat furry body would sprawl across my lap—as if he'd received an engraved invitation to join the queen on her throne.

Snowy knew what it meant to abide. Abiding works under the assumption that you're just supposed to be together. When one walks, so does the other. When one rests, the other snuggles close. It's a picture of what it means to hold fast, remain in, and cling to God.

Picture a coastal pine tree, rooted in the rock, clinging to a rugged bluff on the edge of the Pacific Ocean.

When David thought about his relationship with the living God, he also pictured a deeply rooted tree. In this case, a fruit tree. It's a lovely word picture and worth a closer look.

THE WELL-ROOTED TREE

But his delight is in the law of the LORD,
and on his law he meditates day and night.
He is like a tree planted by streams of water,
which yields its fruit in season
and whose leaf does not wither.
Whatever he does prospers.

PSALM 1:2–3

Root yourself in Him and Him alone. Abide there. Remain in Him. Draw your very life from Him. Cling to Him more tenaciously every day. Some time ago, my dear friend Lori introduced me to a lady who really knew how to abide...and send her roots deeper into the Lord Jesus.

Everyone needs a friend like Lori—someone with a willing ear, an honest heart, and the readiness to go the extra mile with some practical suggestions.

It was at the end of summer, and I was about at my wit's end with my two precious children. I picked up the phone to call my friend-in-need-friend-indeed. "Lori," I said into the receiver, "I think I'm going crazy!"

"Hold on," she said. "Why don't you tell me why you think you *might* be going crazy."

"I just feel so scattered and torn. I'm counting down the days for school to start. Instead of enjoying my kids,

I'm looking for relief! I feel like I should have gotten a management degree just to pull off motherhood, wifehood, and ministry!"

Lori laughed. "You're not crazy. You just need to be still."

What was she thinking? Didn't she hear me explain my chaos? Didn't she realize I was having what I call a "3M" moment? (That's motherhood, ministry, and menstrual.) It's extremely difficult to "be still" in such moments. Even so, I listened to what she had to say. Knowing I was on the emotional edge, Lori gently took over the conversation and began telling me a story I'd never heard before. It was about Susanna Wesley, mother of seventeen.

And about an apron.

Every now and then, when life became too overwhelming, the mother of John and Charles Wesley would sit herself down in a chair and drape her apron over her head. This was her signal that Mom had had enough! Her children—from the least to the greatest—understood they were in dangerous territory if they dared to approach her or disturb her during these times.

Lori went on to explain that Susanna Wesley wasn't just hiding—or maybe practicing Lamaze—under that thin layer of fabric. She was *praying*. She was talking to her Lord about her pressures, her worries, her heartaches, and her need for more of His presence in her life. She was sending her roots just a little bit deeper into the rich riverbank soil of heaven. Simply put, she was clinging to God. In the midst of her busyness, she was abiding in God. While she pulled off her daily rituals, she found a way to remain in Him.

Lori called it "apron therapy" and recommended it to me.

Can't you just imagine this lady's day? Talk about a houseful of kids! It would have looked more like a daycare center gone wild. And there's Susanna in the middle of it all, changing diapers, making meals, sweeping the floor, reading to the little ones, and staggering under mountains of laundry. Now remember, this was in the pre-Maytag, pre-Pampers, pre-Barney, and pre-microwave era—so this was one busy lady! Her life could have so easily been characterized by total and complete chaos—running from task to task, room to room, child to child, and crisis to crisis. She could have been so busy that she had no time to sink her roots into the Lord.

But she made time.

Right in the middle of everything.

In a chair, under an apron.

Everything you read about Susanna Wesley shouts the fact that she made time for the Lord, time to love the Lord her God, listen to His voice, and hold fast to Him.

She rooted herself in God. She drew nourishment and living water, and every day those roots went down just a little bit deeper. In the stillness, she gained strength. Beneath the shadow of the apron, she discovered the shadow of the Almighty and felt the warmth of His embrace. The Lord said it this way: "Be still, and know that I am God" (Psalm 46:10). And David's heart responded: "My soul finds rest in God alone; my salvation comes from him" (62:1). If you and I are going to remain under His touch, we must—just like Susanna Wesley—be still and allow our roots to grow deep. That will only happen as we nestle beneath the shadow of His wing, speaking to Him, singing to Him, meditating on His Word, listening for His voice, and—like Snowy the cat—sticking as near to Him as we possibly can, following Him around wherever He leads.

Though David most likely didn't need an apron to find time to be alone to meditate, he knew the value of keeping an appointment with his God. "On my bed I remember you; I think of you through the watches of the night. Because you are my help, I sing in the shadow of your wings" (Psalm 63:6–7).

Years later, the Lord told His people, "In repentance and rest is your salvation, in quietness and trust is your strength" (Isaiah 30:15).

Don't forget to be still with your Lord. Sink those

roots a little deeper into His love every day. You can abide with Him in stillness even when chaos surrounds you. Remain in His embrace. When we take time to remain, root, and rest in our Father, we find that with each encounter we become just a little more entwined with Him. We draw just a little more of His life. We sense just a little bit more of His sweetness and strength flowing into our branches and leaves, bringing fruit into our daily lives.

Remember that tree planted by streams of water that David wrote about? Because it was well-rooted, because it drank deeply of those fresh, flowing streams, it yielded fruit in season...season after season.

ROOT AND FRUIT

If you came to my home, you would notice lots of pretty green plants dotting my mantel and tables. I even have two beautiful ficus trees, which I pamper and protect from my boys' paper airplanes and Nerf footballs. I love houseplants and indoor trees. In fact, I love them so much that I will not purchase them unless they are made of silk! You see, I don't water my indoor plants; I dust them. I've tried real living plants in my home over the years, but I always end up killing them. Too much water, not enough sunlight, forgetting to repot them before they burst out of the container. Can I just say, my thumb is not green!

I'm no horticulturist, but believe it or not, I have learned a few things about plants and their roots from the Bible. I've learned that there is an unmistakable link between a plant's roots and a plant's fruit. The fruit really is a direct result of the root. The prophet Isaiah knew this well. Look at what he said in Isaiah 37:31: "Once more a remnant of the house of Judah will take root below and bear fruit above." Paul affirms the same truth when he declares that "if the root is holy, so are the branches" (Romans 11:16). When we cling to God and sink our roots deep within Him, a direct result will be sweet fruit growing from our lives.

When Jesus invited His followers to remain in Him, He also included the promise of fruit. He said, "If a man remains in me and I in him, he will bear much fruit" (John 15:5). Just as there is a wide variety of trees, obviously there is a wide variety of fruit. Though the shape, texture, and taste of the fruit may vary greatly, what is certain is that each fruit is a reflection of the root that gives it life. In the same way, each of us as unique individuals will bear fruit with its own special look and feel. But it will be the Root that gives us life. And it will be the result of daily abiding in Him.

Think back through the pages of this book. We've

seen word pictures that illustrate how God has touched people. But now consider how each of those individuals reflected that touch of God through his or her life.

I can't help but think of the woman living in Sychar. She was an arid soul with an empty water jug…until she felt the intimate touch of Jesus. What was the fruit that sprang forth? Most likely it was the salvation of many in Sychar as she overflowed with living water in the town square!

Or what about Jonah? You remember, the man whose prayer closet was in the middle of a fish gut. When God placed His unseen hand upon the disoriented prophet, His guiding touch sent Jonah back on the path of purpose. And what fruit grew out of that touch? At least a generation of Ninevites may have been spared because of Jonah's preaching.

And don't overlook the man who was born blind (John 9), who received the touch of mercy from Jesus Himself. What was the fruit that blossomed? His very life became a canvas that displayed the artful touch of heaven.

I know that you have been touched also. Certainly you have felt His redeeming touch and His touch of mercy. What is your fruit? What shows up in your life as a result of God's tender touch? What has blossomed in your life, wafting the fragrance of His love?

When you remain rooted in Him, when you abide within His embrace, your life will yield sweet, lasting, and satisfying fruit. We are assured by Paul in Galatians 5 that fruit will spring forth and adorn our branches. I pray that we'll have such a bumper crop that our branches won't be able to carry it all! And just like the woman at the well and Jonah, we'll share our fruit with those who need to taste the hope, deliverance, and wild tang of the living God.

For those who are in conflict, may we give the fruit of peace.

For those who mourn, may we offer our joy.

For those injured by hate, may the fruit of love become a healing balm.

For those who have been treated with impatience, let us serve the fruit of longsuffering.

For those who endure harshness, may we graciously extend the fruit of kindness.

For those who have felt the sting of broken promises, may we minister the fruit of faithfulness.

When those around us deserve a sharp word, may we be overcome by the fruit of gentleness. And when the world around us eats the bread of idleness and drinks the wine of folly, may we be sustained by the life-protecting fruit of self-control.

Remain under His touch. Linger there. Walk arm in

arm with Him. Love the Lord; listen to Him; hold fast to Him. When you wrap who you are around who He is, you will become deeply rooted in Him. As you remain, the fruit will explode out of your yielded life.

And that, my friend, is worth passing on.

EIGHT

Passing His Touch Along

Sometimes God's touch comes in an improbable package.

What if it comes in an unexpected moment from an unexpected direction and an unlooked-for source? Would you recognize God's touch if it didn't look or feel anything like you expected? I'm convinced that the more we walk in moment-by-moment fellowship with Him, the more we learn to value the surprising and often unorthodox methods He uses to care for the needs of His kids.

Not long ago I was traveling alone to Tallahassee, Florida. My flight was scheduled to arrive at 2:40 p.m. That arrival time would give me just enough of a window to get to the conference where I was to speak at 6:30 that evening. Unfortunately, that window had been slowly closing since I arrived at the airport early that morning. My original flight had been diverted by stormy weather, and the following two reroutes I'd been booked on both canceled within five minutes of their scheduled departures.

To say things weren't going well would be a gross understatement. I tried not to think of that auditorium in Tallahassee. In a matter of mere hours, it would be filled with expectant people who'd come from who-knows-where to hear me speak. And wouldn't you know it, interspersed with all the traveling chaos that day was the fact that my tickets had randomly tagged me to be searched. After being frisked, patted, and "wanded" by more strangers than I could count, I was beginning to feel like a piece of pizza dough. My bags were searched multiple times. I finally had to remove my boots—and what remained of my dignity—and tried to make the best of it. In the meantime, however, the needle on my stress meter was well within the red zone. I had no one to help me, and everything that could go wrong...DID!

Finally, at yet another security checkpoint, I burst

into tears. I don't think those new white-shirted federal employees had ever encountered a physically exhausted, mentally unstable, and emotionally depleted would-be female terrorist before!

In all the confusion and anxiety, however, something began to surface in my awareness. Although I didn't realize it at the time, God's rescue plan was already taking shape. It began with the simple recognition of two voices. I'd heard them at each of my rerouted gates, and by the time I had settled into my seat for the first leg of my flight, I heard them again. Right behind me.

You can tell quite a bit about people from their conversation. I knew these were two young businessmen traveling together for work. I knew they were trying to get to Tallahassee, just like me. I knew they had taken about all the frustration they could handle. And from their choice of vocabulary, I was pretty certain they weren't missionaries on furlough! (They weren't completely heathen in their language; some words they used were definitely in the Bible.... I'll let you think about that!)

But I was far from judgmental at that point. To tell the truth, I understood just how they felt, and they did seem like good guys. They just had rough wrappings. I turned in my seat and peered into the aisle back toward them.

"I noticed you're trying to get to Tallahassee," I said.

They made a quip and acknowledged that, yes, they were *trying*. I told them I was, too—and that I was desperate to get there.

"I travel alone all the time," I told them, "but I don't have time to wait for assistance from the airlines to transport me to my next gate. I promise you," I assured them, "I can walk as fast as any sighted person on this plane. Will you please let me tag along with you so I'll get there on time?"

They chuckled and consented. This was certainly a wrinkle in their day they'd never expected. We made introductions; my new friends were Jake and Aaron. They were ready and willing to help, and I was ready to make tracks to Tallahassee! Not more than five minutes after Northwest flight 3809 touched down, my two guiding angels and I were plunging through the crowds en route to our gate. I had grasped Jake's arm, while Aaron pulled my bag behind him. We glided the length of two moving sidewalks, deftly maneuvered through the hordes of fellow travelers, and arrived at the gate—just in time!

The line had already formed for boarding. We queued up just as the announcement came through the loudspeakers: Boarding would be delayed due to maintenance issues. Exhaling a collective sigh, we sat down and began to visit.

They were the nicest guys. Their vocabulary was sterilized and well mannered as we talked. Finally we were interrupted by a boarding announcement. *Yes!* We would make it in time! I called the lady in charge of my evening event and told her I would certainly arrive by 7:30. Grateful and relieved, she implemented her Plan B—you know, sing longer and serve more food while you wait for the speaker to arrive!

As we waited to board, however, I sensed the line begin to melt away ahead of us. We were being turned away. That fact was confirmed by the announcement that our flight was *again* delayed—this time due to flight crew issues. At this point, we all began to take issue with the airline's "issues"!

As we headed back to our seats, Jake asked if I would like him to walk me to the ladies' room. *Thoughtful man.* "Yes!" I exclaimed, enjoying the luxury of being escorted directly to the right door. I had no sooner negotiated my way into a stall and unbuttoned my pants when I heard the announcement: "Flight 3840 now ready for *immediate* departure."

"That's me!" I yelled. I yanked open the stall door and ran toward the exit. I was in such a hurry I failed to fasten the top button of my pants! My bladder was about to explode and my pants were sagging, but I made it to the door and screamed, *"JAKE!"*

A large, lumbering man—Jake, I hoped—ran toward me, grabbed my hand, and whisked me into the boarding line once again. As we stood panting, fumbling for IDs, he said, "You *screamed* at me!" His friend Aaron bent over in laughter.

"I'm sorry," I said. "It was just instinct. I knew I needed my traveling angel." We boarded and then parted ways after the flight. And yes, I did finally button my pants.

Unhappily, I never made it to Tallahassee in time to speak. Even so, the experience had its compensations. I received a gift on that journey…two, actually. They were wrapped pretty roughly and their language was coarse, but my two heathen angels became the hand of God that pulled me through airports and met my every need on a most difficult day. (Pray with me for Aaron and Jake. They need to book the one and only flight to heaven through Jesus Christ.)

God can use any means He chooses to help His children and further His purposes.

- He can use a talking donkey to restrain a prophet's madness (2 Peter 2:15–16).
- He can use a storm and a shipwreck to direct His apostle to a peaceful winter refuge (Acts 27:13–28:10).

- He can use the town prostitute to hide and shelter His servants from the enemy (Joshua 2:1–21).
- He can use a rough city jailer to feed His missionaries and tend their wounds (Acts 16:22–36).

We sometimes mistakenly believe that God will use only saints or angels to touch and direct our lives, but that isn't so. When we need the touch of God, He sends it in whatever package He deems best. Sometimes that means we'll be touched by those whom we might normally shy away from, and might be a little uncomfortable around. But stop and think about it: Who were those that touched Jesus when He walked here on earth?

Consider Him for a moment. Jesus, our holy Savior, allowed Himself to be touched by those who were less than holy. Think about the prostitute in Simon's house, who bathed His feet with her tears, wiped them with her hair, and covered them with her kisses.

The outwardly righteous Simon was repelled, but not Jesus.

Think of the ceremonially unclean woman with the issue of blood who crept up behind Him and touched the hem of His robe.

The buttoned-down Pharisees would have been shocked that He allowed Himself to be touched by this woman. But Jesus commended her faith, celebrated her healing, and sent her on her way.

He reached out and made contact with a leper, the lowest of the low—an act that must have horrified even His disciples (Luke 5:13).

Throughout His ministry, Jesus was touched by the common and the lowly, the despised and forsaken. In His final earthly act of humble submission and boundless love, He allowed Himself to be touched by cruel Roman guards. He received their slaps, blows, and lashes, wore their crown of thorns, and felt the pierce of their nails.

Because Jesus allowed Himself to be touched, we are now changed by His touch. We must always look for His touch in our lives. It may come through the heathen, the holy, or even heartache. But once we recognize His touch, we must receive it. Then we can pass it on to someone who desperately needs it.

BECOMING HIS HANDS

God can use unlikely hands to administer His care, provision, and love. Interestingly enough, two of those hands might reside at the end of your arms. If you desire to be used and you're willing to be stretched, *you* might become that unexpected, unlooked-for touch of blessing in someone's life. Maybe even today!

You might say to yourself, *How could I ever make a*

difference in her *life?* Or, *How could God use me to touch* him? You might be surprised.

As I was making spaghetti sauce one afternoon, I felt the nudge of the Holy Spirit. Maybe that sounds strange to you. I wasn't in church. I wasn't at some mountain retreat. I wasn't at a ladies' Bible study.

My hands were going through the familiar steps of creating sauce for our pasta, when the Lord suddenly asked me if He could use those hands to touch someone else. What He suggested was that I make enough extra spaghetti to take to our neighbor, who'd just had a baby.

It was going to be awkward, I told myself, because I'd never met her before. How did I even know if she would need or want my spaghetti? My mind flipped through a whole catalog of rationalizations and reasons not to do such a thing. But then I decided to simply obey the voice of the Lord.

I was so *nervous!* Over the years I have become accustomed to public ministry and standing in front of a big audience. Actually, there's a certain safety and anonymity facing hundreds of people. But going one-on-one with a stranger who might reject my witness (or my sauce) was positively frightening!

What would I say? I tried to compose something in my mind for a minute or two—and then the words suddenly came. I knew exactly what the Lord wanted me to say. *"I am bringing you spaghetti because I am a Christian, and God put it on my heart to reach out and bring you dinner and let you know He loves you."*

Since delayed obedience is really the same thing as disobedience, I marched boldly across the street, knocked on the door, and with little eloquence handed her the spaghetti and told her all God led me to say.

As it turned out, she didn't reject my words or my pasta. In fact, she was touched, amazed, and overwhelmed. She told me, with tears in her voice, what just about every new mom says: "I am tired, I am lonely, I am inadequate...." And she also said thank you.

Becoming God's hands brings great reward. Trusting God in an uncomfortable area renews our confidence in His sovereignty. Stepping out on a new limb makes us want, even more, to walk by faith.

Just because something isn't easy or natural for us doesn't mean it's outside our calling. That one woman is no less important than the thousands I may speak to in public ministry. I hope I never get so comfortable in my "ministry zone" that I miss the call of God to touch individual lives. True public ministry cannot occur unless it is a natural extension of private ministry. If you kept a tally as you read through the four Gospels, you would undoubtedly notice that Jesus touched individuals more often than He touched the masses.

So stock up on the Ragu. You never know when God will use it to touch someone's life. When we are willing to become God's hands, we initiate a marvelous cycle of ministry and worship.

Touching the King

In some mysterious way—certainly beyond my comprehension—our touch upon someone's life actually touches the Lord Himself. In Matthew 25:34–40, Jesus shows us that by ministering to others, we minister to Him. Let's look at the amazing word picture Jesus drew.

> "Then the King will say to those on his right, 'Come, you who are blessed by my Father; take your inheritance, the kingdom prepared for you since the creation of the world. For I was hungry and you gave me something to eat, I was thirsty and you gave me something to drink, I was a stranger and you invited me in, I needed clothes and you clothed me, I was sick and you looked after me, I was in prison and you came to visit me.'
>
> "Then the righteous will answer him, 'Lord, when did we see you hungry and feed you, or thirsty and give you something to drink? When

> did we see you a stranger and invite you in, or needing clothes and clothe you? When did we see you sick or in prison and go to visit you?'
>
> "The King will reply, 'I tell you the truth, whatever you did for one of the least of these brothers of mine, you did for me.'"

Our touch to the world touches Jesus in a way that mere words or worship miss. Have you considered that your act of service is really an act of worship? To touch others with compassion is to touch God with consecrated passion. A Wal-Mart supercenter becomes a worship center when you speak kindness into a discouraged employee's heart. Your office becomes an altar when you go the extra mile and turn the other cheek for the sake of your Savior. A neighborhood barbecue can be a portable kneeling bench where you humbly minister praise to God as you cheerfully offer life-giving words to your community.

To really touch the heart of the compassionate Creator we must with compassion touch the hearts of those He created. If we want to express our love to God, we must express His love to people. "The least of these" are not just the homeless and destitute. No, my friend, I'm a member of the "least of these," and so are you.

The ground upon which the rugged cross stood is perfectly level. No class, no tax bracket, no gender is visible from God's viewpoint—and that's the way it should be for you and me, too. We all need to receive His touch...and be ready to pass it along at the first opportunity. Our hands may be those hands that the Lord uses at odd times and in unlooked-for ways. As we are obedient and walk in His Spirit, He will open doors for us to extend His touch to His discouraged sons and daughters, or those who have lost their way.

Seizing Every Opportunity

When He walked the dusty roads of Jerusalem, Jesus not only received touch but also gave His touch freely. In Matthew 19:13–15, Jesus beckoned the little children to come to Him:

> Some children were brought to Jesus so he could lay his hands on them and pray for them. The disciples told them not to bother him. But Jesus said, "Let the children come to me. Don't stop them! For the Kingdom of Heaven belongs to such as these." And he put his hands on their heads and blessed them before he left.
>
> NLT

That's what Jesus did—He touched. And that's just the reason we should, too. When I was in Oklahoma City for a women's event, I learned something about boldness in reaching out to strangers. It happened when I went to lunch with my new friend Jeanie, the pastor's wife of the church that had invited me. Following a few minutes of chitchat, laughter, and the ritualistic reading of the menu, we were approached by a nice young man—our waiter. His name was Pat.

We exchanged greetings and Pat took our order. What happened next took me completely by surprise.

"Pat," Jeanie said, "in a few moments we will pray before we eat. We would love to pray for you. Is there anything you would like us to pray about?"

Pat, speaking as if someone had bestowed some great honor upon him, humbly replied, "Yes, please. My health." What weights and worries was Pat carrying on his heart? What fears had been gripping him that day? Jeanie responded with loving words and assured him of our prayers.

A number of years ago, you could see the letters WWJD on T-shirts and bracelets just about everywhere you'd go. While Jeanie wasn't wearing those letters on her wrist, she wore them in her *actions*. What Would Jesus Do? What if He had sat down for lunch at a restaurant called Charleston's in Oklahoma City? He would have done exactly what she did. He would have beckoned Pat to come to Him. He would have placed His hands on this worried young man and blessed him. Why? Because just like the little children, Pat matters to Jesus.

What a loss to dismiss any opportunity we might have to splash living water into someone's thirsty soul. Jeanie never actually placed her hands on Pat to bless him, but she touched his heart with a surprising invitation and words of hope.

Sometimes becoming His hands means that we make spaghetti for someone. And sometimes touching others means we don't use our hands at all. You touch something deeper than mere skin. Sincere words, thoughtful actions, gentle gestures, and authentic concern extend our lives and our touch well beyond the physical realm. Touch, after all, is more than skin on skin. Touch is heart to heart.

Chocolate Blessings

Shortly before I got up to speak one night in Orlando, one of the event's organizers placed a paper bag in my hands. "This is from one of our ladies who heard you speak last year," she said. "She's a single mom and she received a scholarship to be here tonight."

I was moved by the thoughtfulness but was in such a

hurry I didn't have the chance to even look in the bag right then. I went into the auditorium, handed my husband the gift bag, and prepared to speak. After a full evening, we packed up and flew home the next day.

Three days later I began to unpack. I walked into my office, dreading what I would find. Cases of books were sprawled across the floor. Half empty CD boxes were perched precariously on top of each other, and the usual stacks of mail and paperwork littered my desktop.

When it comes to my messy office, I'm a total believer in denial, procrastination, and avoidance! I know psychologists would think I'm unhealthy, but they might change their minds if they walked into my office. It looks this way because my husband is not a total believer in garbage cans and their significant influence on one's (namely my) mental health. I call him "Hurricane Phil," because (bless his heart) he really does leave destruction in his wake!

So, as I surveyed the damage before me, I fell back immediately into the warm familiarity of avoidance. *The gift!* I thought. *I wonder what was in that gift bag?* As I began to search for it, I pressed the start button on the CD player, and a beautiful tenor voice began to sing the name of Jesus. My thoughts were immediately drawn to my Savior and His loveliness. Just then I found the bag. I pulled out the tissue paper and reached in. What I pulled out caused my eyes to well up with tears. It was a gift from a single mom who took the time to tell me she was thinking of me. Two boxes of chocolate Sno-Caps.

Now that may seem ordinary and meaningless to you, but this kind lady knew—based on a story I told a year earlier—that Sno-Caps are my very favorite candy. For those few moments, as I held her gift, I was no longer overwhelmed by my messy office. Instead, I became overwhelmed by the sweetness of God, sent to me in a crumpled gift bag by a woman who had little time and money yet spent both on me.

"Your name is like honey on my lips." The lyrics of the CD filled my office and—more importantly—my heart. His name is sweet, His touch is kind and personal, and His timing is always perfect. I know the Sno-Caps came from an anonymous woman in Orlando, but as far as I'm concerned, they came from the hand of God. With the eyes of faith, I could see His invisible fingerprints all over them.

Oftentimes we pray and plead for God's encouragement, wisdom, and blessing. But then when He answers, when His touch truly comes upon our lives, we don't recognize it because it didn't arrive in the expected package. It didn't come to us in the way we anticipated or imagined. Sometimes it comes through the hand of a heathen angel, an average jar of Ragu, a simple prayer, or even a box of chocolates from the hand of a lady who probably needed encouragement more than I did.

Have you felt His merciful touch, like the caress of a cool shadow on a long hot day? Have you felt His strong hand lifting you out of darkness and failure and despair? Have you felt the pressure of His fingers shaping you into someone who will reflect His glory for all eternity?

What you have received, my friend, you can also give. So offer yourself to others. Your time. Your listening ear. Your carefully chosen words of encouragement. Your acts of help and kindness. When you do, you become His touch. His touch shelters. His touch honors. His touch guides. And His touch restores. It may be within the hour. It may be in the middle of the night. It may be in a way you never anticipated, expected, or even considered.

But yours is the skin He chooses, and yours will be the life He uses.

Let's Keep in Touch

I would love to hear how God has touched you, and I invite you to visit me at my website or e-mail me.

On my website you can find information about my other books, Bible studies, and music albums. You can also learn about *Women's Ministry Association, International*—a community you can join to find support, ideas, and resources for women's ministry.

Remember, my friend, "The works of his hands are faithful and just; all his precepts are trustworthy. They are steadfast for ever and ever, done in faithfulness and uprightness. He provided redemption for his people; he ordained his covenant forever—holy and awesome is his name" (Psalm 111:7–9).

May you always recognize His unseen hand and pass along His touch to others.

JR@jenniferrothschild.com
www.JenniferRothschild.com
www.WomensMinistry.NET